S0-AQL-081

Cooking with Grains

Coleen and Bob Simmons

BRISTOL PUBLISHING ENTERPRISES
San Leandro, California

a nitty gritty® cookbook

©1999 Bristol Publishing Enterprises, Inc., P.O. Box 1737, San Leandro, California, 94577. World rights reserved. No part of this publication may be reproduced in any form, nor may it be stored in a retrieval system, transmitted, or otherwise copied for public or private use without prior written permission from the publisher.

Printed in the United States of America.

ISBN 1-55867-221-4

Cover design: Frank J. Paredes
Cover photography: John A. Benson
Food styling: Susan Massey
Illustrations: Shanti Nelson

Contents

A Modern Look at Grains

In 1990, the USDA revamped its dietary guidelines. The new system is represented graphically by a "food guide pyramid." Refined and upgraded in 1995, the diet based on the food guide pyramid is balanced and sensible. As its foundation, the guidelines recommend grain products, such as bread, cereal, rice and pasta, and suggest daily servings of fruits and vegetables to round out meals. Meat, dairy products, fats and oils should be served sparingly.

In line with the food guide pyramid recommendations, this book attempts to provide interesting recipes to help you incorporate more grains into your diet. This is not a vegetarian cookbook, although many of the recipes are meatless. Our main goals were to use grains in recipes that taste good and to utilize some of the less familiar grains on the market today.

Tips for Cooking with Grains

As we developed recipes for this book, we learned some basic techniques for, and information about, grains that we would like to pass along to make your cooking adventures easy and delicious. Following are some suggestions.

- Purchase grains from a high-volume source, particularly if you buy them in bulk. Seek out the best health food store or ethnic market in your area. Or, purchase grains through a reputable mail-order source. A short list appears on page 3.

- Buy only the amount of grains you need or think you will use within 2 to 3 weeks. Whole grains, which still have the germ intact, turn rancid quickly.

- Store grains and grain flours in a cool dark place, preferably in glass jars or plastic containers with tight-fitting lids. In warm, humid climates, store grains in the refrigerator or freezer. Check grains and flours periodically for insects and immediately discard any with signs of infestation.

- Grains have varying moisture contents. Testing and tasting them while cooking is the best way to assure that grains are properly cooked. Older, drier grains usually take longer to cook than do younger, moister ones. All cooking times in this book are approximate.

- An electric crockery pot is a very useful tool for cooking whole grains, particularly those that require long soaking and cooking times. Most grain berries cook from start to finish in 3 to 4 hours in a crockery pot without soaking. Experiment with your model to determine cooking times.

- Cook grains in quantity when you have time and refrigerate them for up to 2 days or freeze them in airtight containers. It is easy to put together recipes when you already have cooked grains on hand.

Mail-Order Sources for Grains and Grain Products

Following is a list of suppliers for hard-to-find grains and grain products:

The Baker's Catalog
P.O. Box 876
Norwich, VT 05055-0876
(800) 827-6836
Specialty flours, baking equipment

Bob's Red Mill Natural Foods, Inc.
5209 SE International Way
Milwaukie, OR 97222
http://www.bobsredmill.com
(503) 654-3215
Organic grains and flours

Dean & DeLuca
http://www.dean-deluca.com
(800) 999-0306
Whole grains and specialty flours

Indian Harvest
P.O. box 428
Bemida, MN 56619-0428
www.indianharvest.com
(800) 294-2433
Wild rice and grains

Lundberg Family Farms
5370 Church Street
P. O. Box 369
Richvale, CA 95974-0369
(530) 882-4551
http://www.lundberg.com
Specialty rices

Basic Stocks for Cooking Grains

About Stocks

Wholesome, flavorful stocks provide a good foundation for cooking grains. Most grains by themselves have a very neutral flavor, but it can be enhanced with aromatic vegetables, spices and flavorful cooking liquids, such as stocks.

Stocks can be made with any combination of vegetables, but the basic flavoring agents are carrots, celery and onions. Use strong-flavored cabbage, turnips and rutabagas in moderation, if at all. It is fine to use vegetables from the refrigerator bin that are a little past their prime, but don't use anything that you wouldn't eat if cooked. It isn't necessary to peel vegetables for use in stocks; just trim them, scrub them and roughly chop them into ¾- to 1-inch pieces. Reducing the stock volume after straining out the solids will intensify the flavor.

Vegetable stock can reflect the seasons. Use zucchini, tomatoes and other summer vegetables when plentiful. Winter flavors are enhanced with a few fresh or dried mushrooms, celery root or chunks of hard-skinned orange squash. Most vegetable stocks can be made in an hour. Further cooking (after the vegetables have released all their flavor) will not produce a stronger-tasting stock.

Basic Beef Stock

Homemade beef stock adds a terrific flavor to soups and sauces and it is well worth the time and effort needed to make your own. It is easy to make home-made stocks: just brown the bones and vegetables in the oven, put them in a pot with water and let the stock simmer on the back of the stove for several hours while you are doing something else. You can make the stock ahead of time and freeze it in convenient portions for later use.

5 lb. beef soup bones, preferably with a small amount of meat attached
3 medium onions, quartered
4 carrots, cut into 1-inch pieces
2 stalks celery with leaves, cut into 1-inch pieces
8 black peppercorns
3 tbs. tomato paste

Heat oven to 450°. Wipe bones with a damp paper towel and place in a low-sided roasting pan or sturdy rimmed baking sheet. Brown bones in oven for 45 minutes, turning once. Add onions and carrots to pan and continue to roast for 15 to 20 minutes, until vegetables are browned; check to see that vegetables do not burn. Place browned meat, onions and carrots in a large stockpot with celery, peppercorns and enough cold water to cover meat and vegetables. Pour off fat from roasting pan and discard. Add about 1 cup water to roasting pan and scrape up the browned bits from pan with a spatula. Add to stockpot. Bring stock to a boil over high heat, skimming and discarding any foam that rises to the top. Reduce heat to low and simmer slowly for at least 4 hours.

Strain stock through a fine sieve into a clean pot. Discard solids. Cool stock rapidly by placing pot in a sink filled with ice water and stirring frequently until cooled to at least room temperature. Cover stock and refrigerate overnight.

Remove and discard any congealed fat on the surface of chilled stock. Bring stock to a boil over high heat. Stir in tomato paste, reduce heat to low and simmer until stock is reduced to about 6 cups. Cool and refrigerate for 3 to 4 days or freeze until ready to use.

Stock can be reduced even further if you want a very rich, concentrated broth, or if freezer space is at a premium. Add a little water to bring up the volume when using for soup or other recipes.

Basic Chicken Stock

When chickens are on sale, buy 3 or 4. Cut them up and freeze the breasts for a quick stir-fry or sautéed chicken entrée. Marinate the legs in your favorite teriyaki sauce and bake them for a picnic or lunchbox. Reserve the wing tips for the stock and marinate the wings in a zesty barbecue sauce before grilling. The rest of the chicken, except for the liver, goes into the stockpot. Each time you cook a chicken, save and freeze the uncooked necks and trimmings. Soon there will be enough chicken parts to make a delicious pot of stock. The frozen parts don't have to be thawed before putting them in the stockpot. Onion and carrot peels give the stock a rich color and flavor.

4-5 lb. chicken parts, carcasses, bones, hearts and/or gizzards
1 large onion, unpeeled
2 large carrots, unpeeled, cut into 1-inch pieces
2 large stalks celery with leaves, cut into 1-inch pieces
2 large sprigs fresh parsley with stems
6-8 black peppercorns
1 bay leaf

Place chicken parts in a large stockpot with enough cold water to cover chicken by at least 2 inches. Bring stock to a boil over high heat, skimming and discarding any foam that rises to the top. Add remaining ingredients and bring back to a boil. Reduce heat to low and simmer slowly for 3 to 4 hours.

Strain stock through a fine sieve into a clean pot. Discard solids. Cool stock rapidly by placing pot in a sink filled with ice water and stirring frequently until cooled. When stock is at room temperature, cover and refrigerate overnight.

Remove and discard any congealed fat on the surface of chilled stock. Bring stock to a boil over high heat, reduce heat to low and simmer until stock is reduced to about 10 cups. Cool and refrigerate for 3 to 4 days or freeze until ready to use.

Stock can be reduced even further if you want a very rich, concentrated broth, or if freezer space is at a premium. Add a little water to bring up the volume when using for soup or other recipes.

Basic Vegetable Stock

This stock is a perfect foundation for risottos, bean dishes or soups. You can vary the vegetables to suit the dish you are preparing. For example, if you are making a springtime risotto with asparagus and peas, add 5 to 6 asparagus spears to the stock to reinforce the asparagus flavor of the finished dish.

1 medium onion, peeled
2-3 large carrots, scrubbed
2 stalks celery with leaves
1 large leek, well washed
1 medium russet potato, scrubbed
4-5 cloves garlic, smashed
1 jalapeño chile, stemmed and seeded,
   or ¼ tsp. red pepper flakes
1 tbs. vegetable or olive oil

6-8 whole fresh parsley stems
5-6 sprigs fresh thyme
2 bay leaves
4-5 black peppercorns
1 tsp. salt
½ cup dry vermouth or white wine,
   optional
2 qt. water

Coarsely chop onion, carrots, celery, leek, potato, garlic and jalapeño. In a large heavy stockpot, heat oil over medium-high heat and sauté chopped vegetables for 5 to 10 minutes, until lightly browned and fragrant. Add remaining ingredients and bring stock to a boil over high heat. Reduce heat to low and simmer uncovered for 45 to 60 minutes. Strain stock and discard solids. Cool, cover and refrigerate for 3 to 4 days or freeze until ready to use.

Cooking with Wheat

About Wheat

Since the cultivation and consumption of wheat predates written history, it is difficult to determine when it was first eaten. Wheat slowly replaced other local grains as it traveled. As a result, more hardy wheat strains with higher yields were developed over time. Today, almost all diets are based on either wheat or rice.

Wheat is high in fiber and vitamins B and E and it provides some protein. Much of the wheat consumed in this country is in the form of bread or pastry, which are made from highly processed "white" wheat flour. Unfortunately, many of the nutrients in wheat are removed by the milling process.

Following are some common forms of wheat available today:

Wheat berries are whole wheat kernels from which the hull has been removed. Wheat berries have a somewhat meaty texture and are good substitutes for ground meat in recipes. Hard wheat berries come from high-protein "hard" wheat strains. Soft wheat berries come from low-protein "soft" wheat strains. Hard wheat berries take a little longer to cook than soft wheat berries, but they are interchangeable in recipes.

Cracked wheat is produced by cutting the wheat berry into 2 or 3 pieces. It can be added to breads or used as a substitute for wheat berries or bulgur.

Bulgur is wheat that has been precooked by either steaming or parboiling, after which it is dried, cracked and separated into grades of fine, medium and coarse. Bulgur is easy to cook and its tender, chewy texture makes it perfect for salads, pilafs, savory stuffings and hearty soups. It is also makes a lovely breakfast cereal.

Spelt is an ancient form of wheat that has a high protein content. Spelt berries are interchangeable with wheat berries.

Couscous is a type of tiny pasta that is made from wheat flour. Traditional couscous is made from cracked semolina, a strain of hard wheat. Couscous is a versatile grain and cooks quickly. In North Africa couscous is used as the base for a dish of the same name, in which the couscous is steamed in a "couscousiere" over an aromatic meat and vegetable stew. The quick-cooking couscous found in markets generally steams in 5 minutes in boiling liquid. Couscous is excellent as a side dish or in a salad.

Israeli couscous is a wheat product with "kernels" about the size of peppercorns. It can be cooked like risotto or boiled like pasta and served topped with a sauce or tossed into a salad. Look for Israeli couscous in a Middle Eastern market or specialty food store.

Basic Soaked Bulgur or Cracked Wheat

*Bulgur and cracked wheat have a toasty, nutty flavor. Soaked bulgur or cracked wheat are usually used for cold dishes like **Tabbouleh Salad**, page 22.*

1 cup fine-, medium- or coarse-grained bulgur, or cracked wheat
cold water or stock if using fine-grained bulgur
boiling water or stock if using medium- or
   coarse-grained bulgur, or cracked wheat

Place bulgur in a bowl and cover with cold or boiling water. Let stand for 30 minutes; drain. Fluff grains with a fork.

Basic Cooked Bulgur or Cracked Wheat

Cooked bulgur or cracked wheat are usually used for hot dishes or when you need it quickly. Cooking bulgur or cracked wheat takes about half as long as soaking it, but it will take extra time to cool if you are using it in a cold dish.

about 2 cups water, stock or other flavored liquid
1 cup fine-, medium- or coarse-grained bulgur, or cracked wheat

Place water in a saucepan and bring to a boil. Add bulgur, reduce heat to low and simmer for 15 to 20 minutes; drain. Fluff grains with a fork.

Basic Cooked Wheat Berries

Like dried beans, wheat berries must be soaked before they are cooked. The texture of cooked wheat berries is similar to fresh corn. Do not add salt during cooking or it could toughen the berries or lengthen the cooking time.

1 cup hard or soft wheat berries   3½ cups cold water, plus water to cover

Place wheat berries in a large bowl and cover with water. Let stand covered overnight; drain. *Quick Soak Method*: Place wheat berries in a saucepan, cover with water and bring to a boil. Remove from heat and let stand for 1 hour; drain.

In a saucepan, bring 3½ cups water to a boil over high heat. Add soaked wheat berries. Reduce heat to low, cover and simmer for 55 to 60 minutes, until tender.

Basic Cooked Spelt Berries

Spelt has a delicious, nutty flavor and more protein and B vitamins than wheat.

1 cup spelt berries   3 cups cold water, plus water to cover

Place spelt berries in a large bowl and cover with cold water. Let stand covered for at least 6 hours or overnight. *Quick Soak Method*: Place spelt berries in a saucepan, cover with water and bring to a boil. Remove from heat and let stand for 1 hour; drain.

In a saucepan, bring 3 cups water to a boil over high heat. Add soaked spelt berries. Reduce heat to low, cover and simmer for about 45 minutes, until tender.

Quick-Cooking Couscous

Makes about 3 cups

Look for couscous that's labeled "instant."

1½ cups boiling water or stock
1-2 tbs. butter

1 cup quick-cooking couscous

Combine ingredients in a saucepan, cover pan and let stand for 5 minutes. Remove lid and fluff grains with a fork.

Basic Cooked Israeli Couscous

Makes about 2 cups

Like pasta, Israeli couscous must be tasted during cooking to judge whether or not it is done. Serve it as a base for vegetable or meat stews, or cool it for a salad or pilaf. You can vary this recipe by adding spices and herbs to the liquid.

1 tbs. olive oil or butter
½ cup finely diced onion, optional
1 cup Israeli couscous

1½ cups boiling water or stock
¼ tsp. salt

In a medium skillet, heat oil over medium heat. If desired, add onion and sauté for 5 to 6 minutes, until softened. Add couscous and stir for 1 to 2 minutes, until grains are coated with oil. Add water and salt. Cover pan, reduce heat to low and simmer for 8 to 10 minutes, stirring occasionally. Remove from heat and let stand covered for 5 minutes. Fluff grains with a fork.

Spiced Breakfast Bulgur

Hot bulgur with dried fruit and spices makes a great breakfast cereal.

1 cup medium-grained bulgur
2½ cups milk, plus more for serving
pinch salt
3 tbs. honey, plus more for serving, optional
½ cup raisins, dried cranberries or dried apple pieces
½ tsp. cinnamon
sugar for serving, optional

In a large saucepan, combine bulgur, milk, salt, honey, raisins and cinnamon and bring to a boil. Reduce heat to low and simmer for 20 minutes, until mixture thickens, stirring frequently. Pour into serving bowls and pass milk and honey or sugar.

Corn and Bulgur Frittata

This colorful frittata makes a great brunch dish or lunchbox treat. Use fine-grained bulgur for this dish. Soak the bulgur while preparing the rest of the recipe ingredients. Other cooked grain berries, such as pearl barley or spelt, can be substituted for bulgur.

about 1 cup *Basic Soaked Bulgur or Cracked Wheat*, page 14
1 tbs. plus 2 tsp. olive oil
½ cup finely chopped onion
kernels from 1 ear fresh corn, about ½ cup
1 small zucchini, trimmed, cut in half lengthwise and thinly sliced
1 small tomato, peeled, seeded and chopped
salt and freshly ground pepper to taste
7 large eggs
3-4 drops Tabasco Sauce
2 tbs. chopped fresh parsley
2 tbs. freshly grated Parmesan cheese

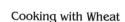

Drain bulgur, squeeze dry and set aside. In a large skillet, heat 1 tbs. of the olive oil over medium heat and sauté onion for 6 to 8 minutes, until softened. Add corn, zucchini, tomato, soaked bulgur, salt and pepper and mix well. Cook for 2 to 3 minutes. Remove from heat.

Heat oven to 450°. In a large bowl, beat eggs, salt, pepper, Tabasco and parsley with a fork until well mixed. Add sautéed vegetables and mix well. Heat remaining 2 tsp. oil in an ovenproof 10-inch nonstick skillet. Pour egg mixture into heated skillet and cook until eggs start to set. Tilt pan and, with a fork, pull eggs from around sides of pan so uncooked portion flows under cooked portion. When top of eggs is no longer liquid, sprinkle with Parmesan cheese and place in oven for 5 to 8 minutes, until top is firm and lightly browned.

Remove skillet from oven, invert a plate on top of skillet and flip frittata onto plate. Invert a serving plate on top of frittata and flip again onto serving plate. Blot any excess oil from surface with paper towels. Cut into wedges and serve warm or at room temperature.

Garden Vegetable Soup

For this soup, substitute the freshest vegetables from your summer farmers' market, such as asparagus, corn, yellow squash or other vegetables. This soup keeps well in the refrigerator for several days.

2 tbs. butter
1 tbs. full-flavored olive oil
1 large or 2 small leeks, white part only, well washed and thinly sliced
2 large carrots, peeled and cut into ½-inch dice
1 large stalk celery with leaves, thinly sliced
4 oz. green beans, stemmed and cut into ½-inch pieces
2 medium zucchini, trimmed, cut in half lengthwise and thinly sliced
2 cloves garlic, minced
1 jalapeño chile, stemmed, seeded and finely chopped
½ cup medium-grained bulgur

4 large tomatoes, peeled, seeded and chopped, or 1 can (14 oz.) ready-cut tomatoes
2 cups *Basic Chicken Stock*, page 8, or canned chicken broth
4 cups water
2 sprigs fresh parsley
3 sprigs fresh thyme
1 bay leaf
1 tsp. salt
freshly ground pepper to taste
1 cup fresh or frozen peas
1 can (15 oz.) cannellini, garbanzo or other beans, rinsed and drained
chopped fresh basil for garnish
freshly grated Parmesan cheese

In a large stockpot, heat butter and olive oil over medium-high heat. Add leeks, carrots, celery, green beans, zucchini, garlic and jalapeño and sauté for 3 to 4 minutes. Add bulgur, tomatoes, chicken stock, water, parsley, thyme, bay leaf, salt and pepper and bring to a boil over high heat. Reduce heat to low and simmer partially covered for 25 to 30 minutes.

Remove and discard parsley, thyme and bay leaf. Add peas and beans. Adjust seasonings and cook soup for 5 minutes to heat through. Serve in hot soup bowls garnished with fresh basil. Pass Parmesan cheese.

Tabbouleh Salad

Serve this lemony Middle Eastern bulgur and herb salad with lettuce or Belgian endive leaves for scooping. It is a nice accompaniment to grilled meats. To save time, wash and dry parsley in a salad spinner and chop it with a food processor. For a delicious variation, stir 1 cup chopped, peeled and seeded tomatoes and 1/2 cup diced cucumber into the finished salad.

Basic Soaked Bulgur, page 14,
   medium-grain
1½ cups chopped fresh parsley
¼ cup chopped fresh mint
5-6 green onions, minced
1 clove garlic, minced

grated peel (zest) from 2 lemons
⅓-½ cup lemon juice
¼ cup full-flavored olive oil
salt and freshly ground pepper to taste
⅓ cup pine nuts, toasted, or chopped
   toasted walnuts

Drain bulgur and squeeze very dry with your hands, discarding soaking liquid. Place bulgur in a serving bowl with parsley, mint, green onions, garlic and lemon zest. In a small bowl, whisk lemon juice, olive oil, salt and pepper until mixed. Pour lemon juice mixture over bulgur mixture and toss lightly. Cover and refrigerate for 1 to 2 hours, or serve immediately. Stir in pine nuts just before serving.

Spelt Berry, Walnut and Corn Salad

Walnut oil lends a distinct nutty flavor to this salad. Buy walnut oil in small bottles and refrigerate it after opening to avoid spoiling. Cooked wheat berries or barley are also good in this salad.

2½ cups *Basic Cooked Spelt Berries*, page 15
½ cup cooked corn kernels
½ cup diced roasted red bell pepper
½ cup chopped toasted walnuts
1 jalapeño chile, stemmed, seeded and finely minced
5 green onions, white part only, minced
2 tbs. chopped fresh parsley
salt and freshly ground pepper to taste
3 tbs. walnut oil
1 tbs. sherry vinegar

In a large bowl, combine spelt berries, corn, red pepper, walnuts, jalapeño, onions and parsley and mix well. Season with salt and pepper. In a small bowl, whisk walnut oil and sherry wine vinegar together; pour over salad and toss well. Check seasonings and serve.

Moroccan Couscous Salad

Serve this cool salad of oranges, cucumber and mint on a warm day. Salting the cucumbers and letting them drain for 20 minutes removes excess moisture. For a decorative presentation, line a platter with leafy lettuce and spoon the salad over the leaves.

1 medium cucumber, peeled, seeded, cut in half lengthwise and thinly sliced
1 tsp. salt
3 cups *Basic Cooked Israeli Couscous*, page 16, room temperature
grated peel (zest) from 1 orange

2 oranges, peeled and thinly sliced
1/3 cup finely chopped red onion
1/4 cup thin ribbons fresh mint
1/4 cup olive oil
2 tbs. lemon juice
1/2 tsp. ground cumin
salt and freshly ground pepper to taste

Place cucumber slices in a colander, sprinkle with salt and drain over a sink for 20 minutes; pat dry with paper towels. In a large bowl, combine couscous, cucumber, orange zest, orange slices, onion and mint. In a small bowl, whisk together olive oil, lemon juice, cumin, salt and pepper. Pour olive oil mixture over couscous mixture and toss to coat grains with dressing. Check seasonings and serve.

Asparagus Couscous Salad

This salad, perfect as a side dish for grilled fish or chicken, can be made ahead of time, refrigerated and brought back to room temperature before serving.

6 cups water
2 tsp. salt
3/4 lb. thin asparagus spears, trimmed
2 tbs. butter
1 1/2 cups quick-cooking couscous
2 tbs. rice vinegar
1 tbs. sugar

1 tsp. finely grated fresh ginger
2 tbs. toasted sesame oil
salt and freshly ground pepper to taste
1/2 cup diced roasted red bell pepper
1/4 cup black or regular sesame seeds, toasted

In a large saucepan, bring 4 cups of the water to a boil. Add 1 tsp. of the salt and asparagus spears and cook for 4 to 5 minutes until crisp-tender. Drain and plunge into a bowl of ice water for 5 minutes; drain and pat dry with paper towels. Cut asparagus into 1-inch diagonal pieces. In a saucepan, bring butter, remaining 2 cups water and 1 tsp. salt to a boil. Add couscous, bring back to a boil and cook for 2 minutes. Cover, remove from heat and let stand for 5 minutes. Fluff grains with a fork and cool for a few minutes. In a small bowl, combine vinegar, sugar and ginger; whisk in sesame oil and season with salt and pepper. Pour couscous into a bowl with asparagus, red pepper and dressing and toss gently. Sprinkle with sesame seeds.

Savory Spinach Tart
with Whole Wheat Crust

A whole wheat crust is the foundation for this zesty spinach, olive and goat cheese filling. Olive paste is available in the specialty food section of most supermarkets. Both crust and filling can be made ahead of time.

2¼ cups whole wheat pastry flour
½ tsp. salt
½ cup plus 2 tbs. full-flavored olive oil
½ cup warm water, 90° to 100°
2 pkg. (10 oz. each) frozen spinach, thawed
1 large onion, chopped, or 2 medium leeks, white part only, well washed and thinly sliced
2 large cloves garlic, minced
⅛ tsp. red pepper flakes

1 tsp. dried thyme, or 2 tsp. fresh
1 tsp. dried sweet basil, or 1 tbs. chopped fresh
3 large eggs
½ cup crumbled feta or fresh goat cheese
2 tbs. black olive paste, or ¾ cup chopped kalamata or oil-cured olives
¼ cup golden raisins
salt and freshly ground pepper to taste
2 tbs. freshly grated Parmesan cheese

Place flour and salt in a large bowl. Add ½ cup olive oil and warm water. Mix with a wooden spoon until dough forms a ball. Wrap dough in plastic wrap and chill in the refrigerator for 1 hour.

Squeeze spinach very dry, blot with paper towels and chop coarsely. In a large skillet, heat 2 tbs. olive oil over medium heat and sauté onion for 6 to 8 minutes, until very soft. Add spinach, garlic, pepper flakes, thyme and basil and cook until mixture is quite dry, about 3 to 4 minutes. Remove from heat, transfer to a large plate and cool for at least 15 minutes. In a large bowl, whisk together eggs, feta cheese, olive paste and raisins. Season with salt and pepper and stir in cooled spinach mixture.

Heat oven to 400°. Place dough between 2 sheets of waxed paper and roll out to an 11-inch circle. Place dough in a 10-inch tart pan and crimp overlapping dough to form a crust. Cover dough with aluminum foil and fill with pie weights or dried beans. Bake crust for 15 minutes. Remove foil and weights and continue to bake for 3 to 4 minutes, until crust feels dry to touch; cool on a rack.

Pour spinach filling into cooled crust and sprinkle with Parmesan. Bake for 25 to 30 minutes, until filling is puffed and lightly browned. Serve warm or at room temperature. Refrigerate tart for 3 to 4 days or freeze. Reheat before serving.

Note: For an excellent baked crust, use a 12-inch Pyrex pizza plate. Or, you can use a tart pan and place it directly on a preheated pizza stone in oven. It is not necessary to prebake crust if using either of these methods.

Stacked Whole Wheat Crepe Sandwich

For a unique lunch dish, whole wheat crepes are layered with an avocado-cheese filling. You can cut this into eighths to serve as an appetizer or snack.

Whole Wheat Crepes

2 large eggs
2 tbs. vegetable oil
1⅓ cups milk
¼ cup fresh cilantro leaves, lightly
    packed

¼ tsp. Tabasco Sauce
1 tbs. brown sugar
½ cup whole wheat pastry flour
½ cup all-purpose flour
½ tsp. salt

To make crepes, process eggs, oil, milk, cilantro and Tabasco with a blender for a few seconds. Add sugar, flours and salt and process on high speed for 20 to 30 seconds. Scrape down the sides of blender container and blend for a few more seconds.

Spray a 6- to 7-inch nonstick skillet with nonstick cooking spray and heat over medium-low heat. When a drop of batter sizzles slightly when dropped in pan, add 2 to 3 tbs. batter, quickly tilting pan to cover entire bottom of pan. Pour any excess batter back into bowl. Cook crepe for about 1 minute.

When top of crepe begins to set and edges look dry or crisp, loosen crepe around edge with a spatula and flip over. If crepe starts to tear when picked up, it may not be cooked enough. Cook crepe for a few seconds on second side.

When done, crepes should have light brown flecks, but still be flexible. Stack cooked crepes on a plate, slightly offsetting them for easier separation. If crepes are made ahead and refrigerated, bring them to room temperature before using.

Filling

1 large ripe avocado
1 tbs. lime juice
salt and freshly ground pepper to taste
4 oz. vegetable-, sun-dried tomato-, or
   herb-flavored cream cheese, softened

1 tbs. milk, optional
½ cup diced, peeled, seeded
   roasted red bell pepper
prepared fresh tomato salsa

To make filling, peel avocado and mash with a fork. Stir in lime juice and season with salt and pepper. Place cream cheese in a small bowl and mix with a spoon until smooth, adding a little milk if needed to achieve a spreading consistency.

To assemble sandwich, place 1 crepe browned-side up on a serving plate. Spread thinly with cream cheese and sprinkle with a few red pepper pieces (it is not necessary to completely cover crepe with red peppers). Top with another crepe and spread thinly with avocado. Alternate filling and stacking until fillings are used.

To serve, cut stack into wedges and spoon a little salsa over the top of each stack. The crepe can be filled and assembled 1 to 2 hours before serving, refrigerated and brought back to room temperature before serving.

Cilantro Pesto Couscous Crepes

Crepes make a distinctive lunch or supper dish. The crepes, couscous and pesto can all be made ahead of time and assembled and heated when you are ready to eat.

about 2 cups *Basic Cooked Israeli Couscous*
    with sautéed onions, page 16
½ cup *Cilantro Pesto*, page 31
½ cup ricotta cheese
10 *Whole Wheat Crepes*, page 28
1 cup shredded Monterey Jack or fontina cheese

Heat oven to 350°. In a bowl, mix warm cooked couscous with pesto and ricotta cheese. Place 1 crepe on a work surface and spread about ⅓ cup of the couscous filling down the center of crepe. Roll up crepe cigar-fashion and place seam-side down in a lightly oiled baking dish. Repeat with remaining crepes and filling. Sprinkle rolled crepes with grated cheese and bake for 20 minutes, until crepes are hot and cheese is melted. Serve immediately.

Cilantro Pesto

*Stir some of this garlicky, brilliant-green pesto into hot cooked couscous or pasta. Or, use it in **Black Bean-Cilantro Pesto Dip**, page 97. An easy way to wash cilantro leaves is to immerse them in a large bowl of cold water, drain them and pat dry on paper towels.*

3 medium cloves garlic
2 cups fresh cilantro leaves, lightly packed (about 1½ bunches)
½ cup fresh Italian parsley leaves, lightly packed
⅓ cup vegetable oil
1 tbs. sesame tahini, or ½ cup slivered almonds, toasted
½ cup freshly grated Parmesan cheese
¼ tsp. salt
freshly ground pepper to taste

Into a food processor workbowl with the motor running, drop garlic cloves through the feed tube and process until finely chopped. Stop motor, add cilantro and parsley leaves and process until finely chopped. Add remaining ingredients and process until well mixed. Transfer to a bowl, cover tightly and store in the refrigerator for up to 3 or 4 days.

Pasta with Tomato-Wheat Berry Sauce

Wheat berries add a meaty texture to this zesty tomato sauce. Start cooking the pasta when the sauce has about 10 minutes left to cook so that the pasta and the sauce will be ready at the same time.

2 tbs. full-flavored olive oil
1 small onion, finely chopped
¼ tsp. red pepper flakes
⅓ cup finely chopped red bell pepper
⅓ cup finely chopped celery
3 cloves garlic, minced
¼ cup finely diced ham, or 2 to 3 thin
    slices prosciutto, finely chopped
2 cans (14 oz. each) ready-cut
    tomatoes
⅓ cup dry red wine

½ tsp. ground anise
1½ tsp. dried oregano
1½ cups *Basic Cooked Wheat Berries*,
    page 15
salt and freshly ground pepper to taste
1 tbs. salt
12 oz. fusilli, orecchiette or other dried
    pasta shapes
2 tbs. chopped fresh parsley
freshly grated Parmesan cheese

In a large skillet, heat olive oil over medium heat and sauté onion, pepper flakes, red pepper and celery for 5 to 6 minutes. Add garlic and ham and cook for 1 minute. Add tomatoes, wine, anise, oregano, wheat berries, salt and pepper. Reduce heat to low and simmer sauce uncovered for 30 minutes, stirring occasionally.

In a large pot, bring 5 to 6 quarts water to a boil over high heat. Add salt and cook pasta according to package directions, draining it about 1 minute before it is completely cooked. Pour drained pasta into cooked sauce and continue to cook for about 1 minute, until pasta is done. Pour pasta and sauce into heated serving bowls and sprinkle with parsley and Parmesan cheese. Serve immediately.

Wheat Berry Stir-Fry

For a quick, hearty late breakfast or lunch, try this Chinese-style stir-fry with wheat berries and any leftover cooked chicken or meat. A fresh fruit salad is the perfect accompaniment.

2 tbs. vegetable oil
4-5 green onions, thinly sliced
dash red pepper flakes
2½ cups *Basic Cooked Wheat Berries*, page 15
1 cup diced cooked chicken, pork or ham
1 large egg, lightly beaten
1 cup peas, thawed if frozen
1 tbs. soy sauce
2 tbs. rice wine or dry sherry
generous grinds black pepper

In a large skillet or wok, heat oil over medium heat. Add onions and pepper flakes and cook for 1 to 2 minutes, until softened. Add wheat berries and chicken and cook for 2 to 3 minutes. Make a well in the center of mixture and pour egg into well; stir with a fork to scramble egg and mix with other ingredients. Stir in peas, soy sauce, rice wine and pepper and heat through. Serve on warm plates.

Spelt Berry Sloppy Joes

These sure kid-pleasers go together quickly if you have cooked spelt or wheat berries in the refrigerator. You won't even miss the meat!

1 tbs. vegetable oil
1 small onion, finely chopped
1 can (8 oz.) tomato sauce
2 tbs. tomato paste
2 tsp. chili powder
1 tsp. dry mustard
1 tbs. brown sugar
2 tsp. apple cider vinegar
½ tsp. celery salt

2 tsp. Worcestershire sauce
½ tsp. Tabasco Jalapeño Sauce,
    optional
freshly ground black pepper to taste
2 cups *Basic Cooked Spelt Berries*
    or *Basic Cooked Wheat Berries*,
    page 15
4-6 small, soft hamburger buns, lightly
    toasted

In a medium skillet, heat oil over low heat. Add onion and cook for 6 to 8 minutes, until soft and lightly browned. Stir in tomato sauce, tomato paste, chili powder, mustard, sugar, vinegar, celery salt, Worcestershire, Tabasco and pepper. Cook over medium heat until bubbling. Add spelt berries, heat through and check seasonings. Serve on hamburger buns.

Curried Chicken with Couscous

You can also serve this spicy chicken over wheat berries, Israeli couscous or bulgur wheat. A fruit salad is a perfect accompaniment. Ghee is clarified butter, which can be found in jars in Indian or Middle Eastern markets.

2 tbs. butter or ghee
8 chicken thighs, skin removed
2/3 cup flour seasoned with salt and
   pepper
1 large onion, chopped
1 large Granny Smith or other tart
   apple, peeled, cored and chopped

1/3 cup golden raisins or dried cranberries
1/2 tsp. dry mustard
1 tbs. Madras curry powder
1 3/4 cups *Basic Chicken Stock*, page 8,
   or canned chicken broth
salt and freshly ground pepper to taste
Quick-Cooking Couscous, page 16

In a large skillet, melt butter over medium-high heat. Roll chicken in flour, brushing off excess. Place chicken in skillet and brown lightly on both sides; transfer to a plate. Reduce heat to low and add onion, apple and raisins; cook for 4 to 5 minutes, until onion is softened and lightly browned. Push mixture to side of skillet and stir in mustard and curry; cook for 1 minute. Gradually add stock to skillet and mix well. Return chicken to skillet, reduce heat to low and simmer covered for 40 to 45 minutes, until chicken is very tender. Adjust seasonings and serve curried chicken over hot couscous.

Rhubarb Crisp

This old-fashioned crisp is still a current-day crowd-pleaser. Organic wheat flakes, not whole wheat breakfast cereal, are used in the crunchy brown sugar topping. If you like, pass a little heavy cream to pour over the top or serve with vanilla ice cream.

1½ lb. rhubarb, trimmed and cut into
   ½-inch pieces
1¼ cups brown sugar, packed
⅓ cup all-purpose flour
1 tsp. cinnamon
2 tbs. Triple Sec or other orange liqueur

5 tbs. butter
¼ cup all-purpose flour
pinch salt
1 cup wheat flakes, rolled oats or
   kamut flakes

Heat oven to 375°. Lightly oil an 8-x-8-x-2-inch baking pan. In a large bowl, toss rhubarb with ¾ cup of the brown sugar, ⅓ cup flour, cinnamon and Triple Sec. In a food processor workbowl, combine butter, ¼ cup flour, remaining ½ cup brown sugar and salt. Pulse several times until butter mixture is the size of small peas. Transfer mixture to a medium bowl and combine with wheat flakes. Pour rhubarb mixture into baking pan and spread evenly. Distribute topping evenly over rhubarb. Bake for 35 to 40 minutes, until topping is lightly browned and rhubarb mixture is bubbling. Serve warm or at room temperature.

Cooking with Barley

About Barley

Like wheat, barley consumption predates written history. Nomadic tribes began cultivating barley first as a cereal grain and soon after as a beer-brewing ingredient. Barley is full of vitamins and is a good source of fiber, complex carbohydrates and protein. Barley is low in fat and has no cholesterol.

While barley has a more distinctive flavor than rice, it, like rice, is a delicious base for soups, stews, salads, curries, casseroles and desserts.

Following are some common forms of barley available today:

Pearl barley is whole-grain barley from which the outer hull has been removed. It is the most common form available. Pearl barley comes in both regular and quick-cooking forms.

Barley flakes make a delicious hot cereal. Cook them as you would oatmeal. Or, use barley flakes in baked goods.

Barley flour is a low-gluten flour. It can be used in baked items to add a distinctive flavor, but it should be combined with wheat flour to achieve the proper results. In general, you can replace up to 25% of the wheat flour with barley flour in yeast breads and up to 50% of the wheat flour with barley flour in cookies and quick breads.

Basic Cooked Pearl Barley

Makes 3½-4 cups

Pearl barley requires no soaking. Take a couple of minutes to sort through it and remove any stones or extraneous materials that may have slipped through the packaging process. Instant or quick-cooking barley usually cooks in 10 to 12 minutes. Follow package directions for specifics.

1 cup regular pearl barley
3 cups water or stock
½ tsp. salt, if using water

Place barley, water and salt, if using, in a medium saucepan and bring to a boil over high heat. Reduce heat to low, cover and cook for about 45 minutes, until barley is tender and most of the liquid is absorbed. Fluff grains with a fork. Cool before refrigerating.

Raisin Scones

These are perfect for a special breakfast or a winter afternoon tea. Oat or millet flour can be substituted for barley flour. Serve with butter and fruit preserves.

1½ cups all-purpose flour
½ cup barley flour
⅓ cup sugar
2 tsp. baking powder
¼ tsp. salt

½ cup butter, cut into pieces
1 large egg, lightly beaten
⅔-¾ cup milk
⅓ cup raisins

Heat oven to 400°. In a large bowl, stir together flours, sugar, baking powder and salt. With a pastry blender or 2 forks, cut in butter until butter mixture is the size of small peas. Add egg and mix well. Gradually add milk and mix until dough is sticky, but workable. Stir in raisins.

On a piece of parchment paper or well-floured work surface, spoon dough into a circle about 1 inch thick. Transfer dough and parchment, if using, to an ungreased baking sheet. With a knife, score dough into 8 wedges. Bake for 25 to 30 minutes, until puffed and golden brown. Cut into wedges and serve hot.

Curried Carrot Barley Soup

This soup can be made in less than an hour if you use quick-cooking barley. Slice the onions and carrots with a food processor for ease.

3 tbs. butter
1 small onion, thinly sliced
pinch red pepper flakes
2 tsp. curry powder
½ cup quick-cooking barley
1 tbs. brown sugar
1 lb. carrots, peeled and thinly sliced

4 cups *Basic Chicken Stock*, page 8,
   or canned chicken broth
1 tbs. lemon juice
salt and freshly ground pepper
plain yogurt for garnish
fresh cilantro leaves for garnish

In a heavy saucepan, melt butter over medium heat and sauté onion for 5 to 6 minutes, until soft. Add pepper flakes and curry and cook for 1 minute. Add barley and brown sugar and cook for 2 to 3 minutes, stirring to coat barley with butter-curry mixture. Add carrots and chicken stock and bring to a boil. Reduce heat to low and simmer covered for 30 minutes, until vegetables are tender. Remove from heat and cool for a few minutes. In batches, carefully puree soup with a blender or food processor and return to pan. Stir in lemon juice, salt and pepper. Serve hot garnished with yogurt and cilantro. If desired, this soup can be cooled and refrigerated for a few days or frozen until needed.

Mushroom Barley Soup

Serve this soup, which freezes well, for a rainy-day meal with hot garlic bread or biscuits. Soaked wheat berries, page 15, can be substituted for barley.

1 oz. dried porcini or shiitake
   mushrooms
6 cups hot water
2 tbs. butter
2 tbs. olive oil
2 large onions, chopped
4 medium carrots, peeled and chopped
1 lb. fresh cremini (brown)
   mushrooms, coarsely chopped

⅔ cup regular pearl barley
4 sprigs fresh parsley
2 sprigs fresh thyme
1 bay leaf
6 cups *Basic Beef Stock*, page 6, or
   canned beef broth
¾ tsp. salt
generous grinds black pepper

Place dried mushrooms in a small bowl with 2 cups of the hot water; let stand for 20 minutes, until softened. Remove mushrooms from liquid and chop coarsley. Strain soaking liquid through a paper coffee filter or cheesecloth and reserve.

In a medium stockpot, heat butter and olive oil over low heat. Add onions and carrots and sauté for 5 to 7 minutes. Increase heat to medium-high, add fresh mushrooms and sauté for 3 minutes. Add barley and cook for 2 minutes. Add parsley, thyme, bay leaf, stock, mushroom liquid and remaining 4 cups hot water. Simmer uncovered for 45 minutes, until barley is soft. Adjust seasonings and serve.

Middle Eastern Barley Salad

For a party, arrange a border of lightly dressed mixed baby salad greens on a platter. Spoon the salad in the middle of the platter and crumble feta cheese over the top. You can substitute cooked bulgur, quinoa or Israeli couscous for barley, if desired.

2 cups *Basic Cooked Pearl Barley*,
   page 40, room temperature
4-5 green onions, white part only,
   thinly sliced
1 medium-sized red bell pepper,
   stemmed, seeded and diced
1 large stalk celery, cut into ¼-inch dice
1 cup diced seeded cucumber
1 cup diced peeled, seeded tomato
⅓ cup chopped kalamata olives
¼ cup capers, rinsed and drained

⅓ cup chopped fresh mint
¼ cup chopped fresh parsley
¼ cup full-flavored olive oil
2 tbs. lemon juice
1 clove garlic, finely minced
½ tsp. dried oregano
½ tsp. ground cumin
salt and freshly ground pepper to taste
½ cup crumbled feta cheese, optional
pita pockets or lettuce leaves
   for serving

In a large bowl, combine cooked barley, onions, red pepper, celery, cucumber, tomato, olives, capers, mint and parsley and toss well. In a small bowl, whisk together olive oil, lemon juice, garlic, oregano, cumin, salt and pepper. Pour dressing over barley mixture and toss well. If desired, sprinkle with crumbled feta cheese. Serve in pita pockets or lettuce leaves. Salad can be made ahead and refrigerated for a few hours; remove from refrigerator at least 30 minutes before serving.

Asparagus Barley "Risotto"

This fresh, light dish is the essence of spring. Serve it as a first course or as a main dish for a luncheon or supper.

1 lb. thin asparagus
4-4½ cups *Basic Chicken Stock*, page 8, or 2 cans
    (14 oz. each) chicken broth plus ½ cup water
2 tbs. olive oil
1 tbs. butter
1 small yellow onion, finely chopped
1 clove garlic, minced
1½ cups quick-cooking pearl barley
¼ cup dry vermouth or white wine
½ cup diced smoked chicken or ham, optional
1 tbs. minced fresh tarragon, or 1 tsp. dried
grated peel (zest) of 1 lemon
2 tbs. lemon juice
salt and freshly ground pepper to taste
⅓ cup freshly grated Parmesan cheese, plus more for passing

Trim and discard tough ends from asparagus. Cut off asparagus tips and reserve. Cut asparagus stalks into ½-inch pieces. Bring a small pot of water to a boil, add asparagus tips and pieces and cook for about 5 minutes, until crisp-tender. Drain, rinse with cold water and set aside.

In a saucepan, bring chicken stock to a boil over high heat. Reduce heat to very low and keep just at a simmer. In a heavy 2- to 3-quart saucepan, heat olive oil and butter over low heat until foaming. Add onions and cook for 4 to 5 minutes, until soft and translucent. Add garlic and barley and stir to coat with oil mixture. Add about 1 cup of the simmering stock and cook over medium heat, stirring occasionally, until stock is absorbed. Add vermouth. Continue to add stock about ½ cup at a time, stirring until barley has absorbed liquid before adding more. Barley should remain at a simmer. After barley has cooked for about 15 minutes, bite into a grain. It should be almost cooked through with just a small firm center; if not, continue to cook.

Stir in chicken, asparagus, tarragon, lemon zest, lemon juice, salt and pepper. Continue to cook for about 5 minutes. Stir in Parmesan and serve immediately in a heated serving bowl or on warm plates. Pass additional Parmesan cheese.

Barley-Stuffed Grape Leaves

This version of Middle Eastern "dolmas" features a filling of quick-cooking barley and mushrooms. These can be made ahead of time and refrigerated for up to 3 or 4 days before serving. Pack them in a brown-bag lunch or serve them as nibblers at a cocktail party.

¼ cup olive oil
1 cup finely chopped onion
1 clove garlic, finely chopped
½ lb. fresh white mushrooms, trimmed and finely chopped
½ cup quick-cooking pearl barley
1 tsp. dill weed
2 tbs. finely chopped fresh mint
2 tbs. finely chopped fresh parsley
salt and freshly ground pepper to taste
¼ cup lemon juice
¾ cup *Basic Chicken Stock*, page 8, or canned chicken broth
1 jar (8 oz.) grape leaves in brine
1½ cups water, plus more if needed

In a large skillet, heat 2 tbs. of the olive oil over low heat and sauté onion for 6 to 8 minutes, until soft. Add garlic and mushrooms, increase heat to medium-high and cook for 3 to 4 minutes, until mushroom liquid is released. Add barley and cook for 3 to 4 minutes, stirring occasionally. Add dill weed, mint, parsley, salt, pepper, 2 tbs. of the lemon juice and chicken stock. Simmer covered for 15 minutes, until most of liquid has been absorbed and barley is almost tender. Remove from heat and cool.

Separate grape leaves and rinse in a bowl of cold water. With scissors, cut off tough stems even with base of leaves. Layer leaves on paper towels to dry.

Place 1 leaf shiny-side down on a plate, stem-end closest to you. Spoon about 1 tbs. of the barley filling just above stem. Fold in the sides of leaf and roll up jelly roll-style. If leaves are extremely large, trim sides and top with a sharp knife to make a neater roll; reserve trimmings. Repeat with remaining leaves and filling. Place stuffed grape leaves seam-side down in a single layer in a large skillet. Top with grape leaf trimmings, if any. Mix remaining 2 tbs. olive oil and 2 tbs. lemon juice with water and pour over filled grape leaves; liquid should come halfway up the side of the rolls. Bring liquid to a boil over high heat. Place a large flat plate or lid over stuffed leaves and cover skillet with another lid. Reduce heat to very low and simmer for 35 minutes. Add more water, if necessary, during cooking. Transfer stuffed grape leaves to a platter, cool and refrigerate. Serve at room temperature.

Orange Barley Pilaf

This pilaf is a delicious accompaniment for grilled fish or roasted chicken.

2 tbs. butter
½ cup finely chopped onion
1 cup regular pearl barley
2 cups *Basic Chicken Stock*, page 8, or canned chicken broth
¼ cup orange juice concentrate, thawed
½ tsp. salt
1 cup coarsely chopped fresh cilantro leaves, lightly packed
¼ cup slivered almonds, toasted

In a heavy 2- to 3-quart saucepan, melt butter over low heat. Add onion and sauté for 3 to 4 minutes, until translucent. Add barley and cook for 3 to 4 minutes, stirring to coat grains with butter. Add chicken stock, orange juice concentrate and salt and bring to a boil. Reduce heat to low and simmer covered for about 35 minutes, until liquid has evaporated and grains are tender. Stir in cilantro, cover and let stand for 5 minutes. Stir in almonds, fluff grains with a fork and serve immediately.

Pork and Barley Stew

Canned green chiles add punch to this hearty lunch or supper dish. Warm flour tortillas are perfect accompaniments.

2 tbs. vegetable oil
1 large onion, diced
4 cloves garlic, minced
1 tbs. ground cumin
1 can (7 oz.) diced green chiles
2 tsp. dried oregano
1½ lb. pork tenderloin, trimmed and
    cut into ⅜-inch cubes
3 cups *Basic Chicken Stock*, page 8,
    or canned chicken broth

4 cups *Basic Cooked Pearl Barley*,
    page 40
salt and freshly ground pepper to taste
cayenne pepper or hot pepper sauce
    to taste
garnishes: fresh cilantro leaves; peeled,
    seeded and diced tomato; diced
    avocado; finely chopped onion;
    shredded Monterey Jack cheese

In a large skillet, heat oil over medium heat and sauté onion for 2 to 3 minutes, until softened, but not browned. Add garlic and cook for 2 to 3 minutes. Stir in cumin, green chiles and oregano. Add pork cubes and stock, reduce heat to low and simmer covered for 30 minutes. Add barley, salt, pepper and cayenne and cook for 10 minutes. Serve in warm soup bowls with your choice of garnishes.

Beef Shanks and Barley

This hearty cool-weather entrée is comfort food at its best! It tastes even better the next day.

2 tbs. olive oil
4 center-cut beef shanks (about 3 to 4 lb. total)
1 large onion, coarsely chopped
1 large carrot, coarsely chopped
1 stalk celery with leaves, coarsely chopped
1 jalapeño chile, stemmed, seeded and minced
2 cloves garlic, cut in half
grated peel (zest) and juice from 1 orange
2 cups water

2 cups *Basic Beef Stock*, page 6, or canned beef broth
1 bay leaf
4-6 black peppercorns
1 cup regular pearl barley
½ cup diced onion
½ cup diced carrot
¼ cup diced celery
¼ cup diced turnip
½ cup dry vermouth or white wine
2 tbs. tomato paste
2 tsp. salt
generous grinds freshly ground pepper

In a large heavy casserole, heat olive oil over medium heat. Wipe beef shanks with a damp paper towel and brown on both sides in olive oil. Transfer shanks to a plate. To casserole, add chopped onion, chopped carrot, chopped celery and jalapeño and cook for 3 to 4 minutes, stirring occasionally. Add garlic and orange zest and cook for 1 minute. Return beef shanks to pan. Add orange juice, water, stock, bay leaf and peppercorns and bring to a boil over high heat. Reduce heat to low and simmer covered for about 1¾ hours, until beef is very tender.

Transfer meat to a plate and strain broth into a bowl through a sieve, pressing solids with the back of a spoon to extract liquid into broth; discard solids. Skim as much fat from broth as possible and pour broth back into casserole. (Beef shanks can be cooled and refrigerated in broth for 2 to 3 days at this point. If broth has been refrigerated, remove any congealed fat that sits on the surface before continuing with recipe.)

Bring broth in casserole to a boil over high heat. Stir in barley, diced vegetables, vermouth, tomato paste, salt, black pepper and beef shanks. Reduce heat to low and simmer covered, stirring occasionally, for about 45 minutes, until barley is tender. Serve in warm soup plates.

Chocolate Barley Nuggets

Tuck these into a lunchbox or serve them with an afternoon cup of tea. For easy cleanup, line baking sheets with parchment paper. You can replace ¾ cup of the all-purpose flour with barley or oat flour, if desired.

2 squares (1 oz. each) unsweetened
   baking chocolate
¾ cup vegetable shortening
1 cup granulated sugar
¼ cup brown sugar, packed
1 large egg
1 tsp. vanilla extract
2 tbs. dark rum or brandy, optional

1½ cups all-purpose flour
1 tsp. baking soda
½ tsp. salt
1 tsp. cinnamon
½ cup buttermilk
1½ cups barley flakes
½ cup chopped pecans

Heat oven to 350°. Melt chocolate in a small bowl over a pan of hot water, or microwave on HIGH for 60 to 90 seconds, stirring after 30 seconds. Cool slightly. With a mixer, beat shortening with sugars until light and fluffy. Add egg, vanilla, rum, if using, and melted chocolate and mix well. In a small bowl, stir together flour, soda, salt and cinnamon. Mix flour mixture into chocolate mixture alternately with buttermilk. Stir in barley flakes and pecans. Drop rounded teaspoonfuls of dough onto baking sheets. Bake for about 15 minutes, or until cookies are firm to the touch. Cool on a rack.

Old-Fashioned Refrigerator Cookies

With this dough on hand in the refrigerator, a panful of crisp warm cookies is only 15 minutes away. Substitute ¾ cup barley or oat flour for part of the all-purpose flour, if desired. Line baking sheets with parchment for easy cleanup.

1 cup butter, softened
1 cup brown sugar, packed
1 cup granulated sugar
2 large eggs
1 tsp. vanilla extract
1½ cups all-purpose flour

1 tsp. baking powder
½ tsp. cinnamon
1 tsp. salt
3 cups barley flakes
½ cup chopped walnuts
½ cup chopped dates or raisins

With a mixer, beat butter with sugars until light and fluffy. Add eggs and vanilla and mix well. In a small bowl, mix flour with baking soda, cinnamon and salt; gradually add flour mixture to egg mixture, mixing well. Add remaining ingredients to bowl and mix well; dough will be sticky. Divide dough in half and place each half on a long sheet of waxed paper. Using waxed paper, shape dough into 2 long rolls, about 3 inches in diameter. Place rolls in the refrigerator until firm, for at least 4 hours.

Heat oven to 350°. Cut cookie dough into ¼-inch slices and place on baking sheets about 2 inches apart. Bake for about 15 minutes, until cookies are lightly browned and firm to the touch. Cool on a rack.

Plum Cake

Barley flour is used in this moist, homestyle fruit-topped cake. A scoop of rich vanilla ice cream is a delicious accent.

½ cup butter
1 cup plus 2 tbs. sugar
2 large eggs
1 tsp. vanilla extract
grated peel (zest) from 1 lemon
½ cup barley flour

½ cup all-purpose flour
1 tsp. baking powder
⅛ tsp. salt
6 medium-sized fresh plums, pitted and
    cut into quarters
½ tsp. cinnamon

Heat oven to 350°. Butter a 9-inch springform pan. With a mixer, beat ½ cup butter with 1 cup sugar until light and fluffy, about 2 minutes. Add eggs, vanilla and lemon zest and mix well. In a small bowl, combine flours, baking powder and salt and whisk to combine. Add flour mixture to egg mixture and beat on high speed for 2 minutes, until batter is stiff and smooth. Spread batter in prepared pan. Arrange plums on top of batter and sprinkle with 2 tbs. sugar and cinnamon. Bake cake for 45 minutes, until cake pulls away from the sides of pan and a toothpick inserted into the center comes out clean. Cool on a rack for 10 minutes. Run a thin knife around the edge of cake and release it from pan. Cool on a rack. Cut into wedges and serve at room temperature.

Cooking with Rice

About Rice

Rice as we know it was most likely developed when wild grasses were domesticated about 5,000 years ago. Rice thrives in warm climates where there is a good water supply. Thousands of varieties of rice are grown around the world. Several imported varieties are now widely available in the United States, including basmati from India, jasmine from Thailand and Arborio from Italy.

Rice is a very important ingredient in the diet of over half the world's population. In many cultures it is consumed 3 times a day. Rice has a fair amount of protein B vitamins, phosphorus and magnesium. Rice can be used to make everything from soups to salads, side dishes, entrées and desserts. It is also manufactured into cereal and flour, as well as a lactose-free milk alternative, which has only 1% fat.

A few of the more common varieties of rice are described below:

Brown rice is whole-grain rice from which the outer husk has been removed. It is more nutritious than white rice and has a nutty flavor. Brown rice takes a little longer to cook than white rice. Although long-grain is the most common type of brown rice, it is also available in medium- and short-grain varieties.

White rice is brown rice that has been stripped of its bran and germ. Due to the stripping process, white rice has fewer nutrients and less fiber than brown rice. The long-grain variety of white rice cooks into soft separate soft separate grains. If the package of rice says "enriched," rinsing or soaking the rice before cooking is not necessary. The rice has already been carefully washed and lightly coated with vitamins and minerals.

Converted rice is white rice that has been steamed before the bran is removed, which preserves some nutrients. The grains remain firmer than regular long-grain white rice, which makes it a good choice to add to long-cooking dishes, such as jambalaya, gumbo and paella.

Basmati rice is an aromatic white rice from India. Its long, tender grains have a distinct earthy aroma. It's great with curries or in pilafs.

Jasmine rice, like basmati, is a type of aromatic white rice with long, separate grains and a distinct perfumy aroma. The best is imported from Thailand. Domestically grown varieties are less aromatic.

Wehani red rice is a California medium-grained hybrid based on an Asian red rice variety. It has a chewy texture and an aroma similar to popcorn.

Arborio rice is a short-grained Italian variety that becomes creamy with constant stirring while cooking. It remains slightly firm after cooking, but absorbs the flavor of the cooking liquid. Arborio is a classic choice for making risotto.

Basic Cooked Brown Rice

If you buy brown rice in bulk, sort through the grains, removing any little stones and other foreign material. Rinse the rice under several changes of cold water before proceeding.

2¼ cups water   1 tsp. salt
1 cup long- or short-grain brown rice

In a medium saucepan, bring water to a boil. Add rice and salt and cover pan tightly. Reduce heat to low and simmer for 30 to 45 minutes. Check a rice grain after 30 minutes to see if it is tender and water has been absorbed.

Basic Cooked White Rice

Makes 3 cups

In general, basmati and jasmine rice use a little less water than white rice, but the technique is the same. Unless the package or rice says "enriched," it is a good idea to rinse the rice under several changes of water until the water runs clear.

1¾-2 cups water   1 tsp. salt
1 cup long- or medium-grain white rice

Follow instructions for *Basic Cooked Brown Rice*, but cook white rice for 15 to 18 minutes; check a rice grain after 15 minutes.

Rice Soup (Congee)

Every rice-based cuisine has a version of this nourishing, easy-to-digest soup. It is often eaten as a late-night snack or for breakfast. Make a large batch of the basic soup and reheat it with different garnishes for weekday breakfasts. Or, add liquid to leftover cooked steamed rice and cook until it is very soft.

3½ cups *Basic Chicken Stock*, page 8, or canned chicken broth
3 cups water, plus more if needed for reheating
1 cup long- or medium-grain rice
thin egg omelet, cut into strips for garnish, optional
thinly sliced green onions or chopped fresh chives for garnish, optional
diced cooked ham, chicken or pork for garnish, optional
soy sauce for garnish, optional
hot pepper sauce for garnish, optional

In a heavy 4-quart saucepan, bring stock and water to a boil. Add rice and return to a boil. Stir mixture and reduce heat to very low. Partially cover pan and simmer slowly for 1½ hours, stirring occasionally. Serve immediately with desired garnishes or refrigerate. Mixture will thicken somewhat during cooling. Thin with a little more water or soy sauce when reheating.

Brown Rice Salad with Tahini-Lemon Dressing

Cool the rice before tossing it with the vegetables and dressing. Sesame tahini is available in Middle Eastern markets or in the ethnic food section of some major supermarkets.

1 yellow crookneck squash or
   zucchini, diced
½ cup diced carrot
½ cup cooked peas
½ cup diced roasted yellow or red bell
   pepper
4 green onions, white part only, minced
about 2 cups *Basic Cooked Brown
   Rice*, long-grain, page 60, cooled
2 tbs. chopped fresh parsley

5-6 fresh mint leaves, cut into ribbons
1½ tbs. lemon juice
1 tbs. rice vinegar
2 tbs. sesame tahini
1 tbs. olive oil
1 tbs. water
½ tsp. ground cumin
salt and freshly ground pepper to taste
5-6 drops Tabasco Sauce

Fill a medium saucepan with water and bring to a boil. Add squash and boil for 1 minute. Remove squash with a strainer and run under cold water to stop cooking. Add carrot to boiling water and boil for 2 minutes; drain and cool.

Place squash and carrot in a large bowl. Add peas, pepper, onions, rice, parsley and mint and mix well. In a small bowl, mix lemon juice, rice vinegar, sesame tahini, olive oil, water, cumin, salt, pepper and Tabasco. Add dressing mixture to rice mixture and mix well. Serve immediately.

Warm Spinach, Mushroom and Brown Rice Salad

Cooked pearl barley or wheat, rye or spelt berries can be substituted for the brown rice. The warm dressing should be poured over the salad just before serving.

4 slices bacon, cut into small pieces
2-3 tbs. olive oil
2 tbs. sherry vinegar
¼ cup dry vermouth or white wine
8 medium cremini (brown) mushrooms, trimmed and thinly sliced
⅓ cup finely chopped red onion

½ tsp. Dijon-style mustard
1 cup *Basic Cooked Brown Rice*, long grain, page 60
6 cups baby spinach leaves, well washed and dried
salt and freshly ground pepper to taste

In a medium skillet, sauté bacon until brown and crisp. Remove bacon from pan and pour out drippings. To skillet, add olive oil, vinegar and vermouth and bring to a boil over high heat. Add mushrooms and onion and cook over low heat for 3 to 4 minutes, until mushrooms and onion are soft. Add mustard and stir until well blended. Add rice and cook for 1 minute, until warmed. Place spinach leaves in a salad bowl and pour hot rice mixture over leaves. Toss, season with salt and pepper and serve immediately.

Classic Risotto

Risotto is typically made with the Italian short-grain rice called Arborio. A medium-grain California rice is an acceptable alternate. Use any of the stocks in the Basic Stocks chapter, or a good brand of canned chicken, beef or vegetable broth.

2½-3 cups stock
2 tbs. full-flavored olive oil or butter, or a combination
1 small onion, finely chopped
1 clove garlic, finely chopped

1 cup Arborio rice
salt and freshly ground pepper to taste
⅓ cup dry white wine or vermouth
3 tbs. finely chopped fresh parsley
freshly grated Parmesan cheese

In a saucepan, bring stock to a boil over high heat. Reduce heat to very low and keep just at a simmer. In a heavy 2- to 3-quart saucepan, heat oil over medium heat. Add onion and sauté for 3 to 4 minutes. Add garlic and rice and sauté for about 2 minutes, until rice is well coated with oil and begins to turn translucent. Add salt and pepper. Combine wine with hot stock. Add about 1 cup of the simmering stock mixture to rice and cook, stirring until liquid is absorbed. Continue to add stock about ½ cup each time, stirring until rice has absorbed liquid before adding more. Rice should remain at a simmer. After rice has cooked for about 15 minutes, bite into a grain. It should be almost cooked through with just a small firm center; continue to cook, stirring, for 2 to 4 minutes, until center is soft, but not mushy. Check seasonings and serve immediately sprinkled with parsley. Pass Parmesan.

Classic Mushroom Pilaf

Aromatic basmati rice is perfect for this side dish, but you can use another type of long-grain rice if you wish. Converted rice remains too firm and will not produce the desired texture for the pilaf. Start soaking the rice about 20 minutes before cooking the pilaf. The green peas can be cooked with the rice, or cooked separately and added just before serving to preserve their bright green color.

1 cup basmati or long-grain white rice
2 tbs. butter or ghee (clarified butter)
1 small onion, quartered and thinly sliced
5 large cremini (brown) or white mushrooms,
   trimmed and cut into matchstick-sized pieces
1 small clove garlic, minced
1/4 tsp. cardamom
1 1/3 cups *Basic Vegetable Stock*, page 10, or canned vegetable broth
1/2 tsp. salt, or less to taste if using canned broth
1/2 cup small green peas, thawed if frozen

Place rice in a medium bowl and rinse in several changes of cold water. When water runs clear, cover rice with cold water by about 1 inch and let stand for 30 minutes. Drain in a sieve and discard soaking liquid.

In a heavy saucepan with a tight-fitting lid, melt butter over medium heat until foaming. Add onion and sauté for 3 to 4 minutes. Add mushrooms and sauté for about 5 to 6 minutes, until mushroom liquid is released and are lightly browned. Add garlic and rice and sauté until rice is well coated with butter and grains begin to turn translucent. Add cardamom, stock and salt and bring to a boil. Stir in peas and return liquid to a boil. Cover pan, reduce heat to very low and simmer for 25 minutes. Do not remove lid during cooking time. Remove pan from heat and let stand covered for 5 minutes. Remove lid and gently fluff grains with a fork; serve immediately.

Stuffed Portobello Mushrooms

Brown basmati rice is very good in this recipe, but cooked pearl barley or wheat berries can also be used. Crumbled cooked bacon or pancetta pieces can be substituted for diced ham, if desired. Serve with hot garlic bread and a crisp green vegetable.

4 large portobello mushrooms, about 4 inches in diameter
2 tbs. olive oil
5-6 cremini (brown) mushrooms, trimmed and chopped
¼ cup finely chopped shallots or onion
1 large clove garlic, finely chopped
1 cup *Basic Cooked Brown Rice*, page 60
salt and freshly ground pepper to taste
6-8 sun-dried tomatoes, chopped
½ cup diced cooked ham
2 tbs. chopped fresh parsley
⅔ cup shredded Monterey Jack cheese
½ cup water

Heat oven to 350°. Twist stems off portobello mushrooms. Trim and chop firm parts of stems and set aside; discard any mushy parts of stems. With a spoon, gently scrape black gills from the bottom of mushroom caps; discard gills.

In a large skillet, heat olive oil over high heat. Add chopped mushrooms and reserved stems and sauté for 2 to 3 minutes, until mushrooms have released their liquid. Reduce heat to medium, add shallots and garlic and sauté for 2 to 3 minutes, until softened. Stir in brown rice and sauté for 1 minute. Season with salt and pepper. Remove skillet from heat and add tomatoes, ham, parsley and cheese; mix well.

Divide stuffing among mushroom caps, mounding it in the center and pressing down firmly. Pour water into a baking pan just large enough to hold mushrooms. Place mushrooms in pan, cover pan with a lid or aluminum foil and bake for 20 minutes. Remove lid or foil and continue to bake for 10 minutes, until mushrooms are lightly browned. Mushrooms are done when a knife blade penetrates them easily. Serve hot.

Wehani Red Rice with Chicken and Sausages

Servings: 6

Rice with chicken and sausage is a classic Spanish combination. The Wehani red rice gives this dish a beautiful brownish-red color and an intriguing aroma. Serve it with a crisp green salad and some hot garlic bread.

1 lb. mild or spicy Italian or chorizo sausage
6 chicken thighs, skin removed
flour seasoned with salt and pepper
2 tbs. olive oil
1 medium onion, finely chopped
1 red bell pepper, stemmed, seeded and cut into ⅜-inch squares
2 cups Wehani red rice or converted white rice
3 cloves garlic, finely chopped
1 tsp. hot Hungarian paprika, or 1 tbs. mild
salt and freshly ground pepper to taste
3-4 cups *Basic Chicken Stock*, page 8, or canned chicken broth
2 large tomatoes, peeled, seeded and coarsely chopped,
    or 1 cup drained canned tomato pieces
1½ cups fresh or frozen peas
¼ cup chopped fresh parsley

Place sausage in a medium-sized ovenproof skillet with water to cover. Bring water to a simmer and cook for 10 minutes, turning sausages over and pricking with a knife to release fat. Drain sausages, cut into ½-inch slices and set aside. Rinse and dry chicken thighs and dust lightly with seasoned flour. In a ovenproof casserole, heat oil over medium-high heat and sauté chicken until browned on both sides and nearly cooked through, about 20 minutes. Transfer chicken to a plate.

Heat oven to 350°. Add onion and red pepper to casserole and sauté for 4 to 5 minutes, until vegetables are softened. Add rice and sauté for 3 to 4 minutes. Stir in garlic, paprika, salt and pepper. Add 3 cups chicken stock and bring mixture to a boil over high heat. Cover casserole, reduce heat to low and simmer for 15 minutes, stirring occasionally, until rice has absorbed some of the liquid. Add chicken thighs and sausage slices, pushing them down into rice. Add tomatoes. Cover casserole and bake for 30 minutes. Remove lid and check to see if rice is tender and chicken is completely cooked. Add a little more stock if mixture seems too dry. Stir in peas and cook uncovered for 10 minutes. Garnish with parsley and serve immediately on warm plates.

Pineapple Rice Pudding

Fragrant jasmine rice pairs with vanilla Rice Dream nondairy beverage for a creamy, guilt-free dessert. Rice Dream is available in most large supermarkets. Since it doesn't require refrigeration until it is opened, look for Rice Dream on the shelf near the canned milk in a 1-quart cardboard carton.

1¾ cups vanilla-flavored Rice Dream
    nondairy beverage
1¼ cups water
pinch salt
¾ cup jasmine rice
⅓ cup sugar

4 oz. egg substitute
1 tsp. vanilla extract
1 can (8 oz.) crushed pineapple with
    juice
1 tbs. dark rum, optional

In a heavy saucepan with a tight-fitting lid, bring 1 cup of the Rice Dream and water to a boil. Stir in salt and rice. Cover pan, reduce heat to very low and simmer for 30 minutes; remove from heat.

In a small bowl, whisk together remaining ¾ cup Rice Dream, sugar, egg substitute and vanilla. Stir pineapple with juice into hot rice. Place saucepan over low heat and stir in egg mixture and rum, if using. Cook, stirring frequently, until mixture simmers and thickens. Remove from heat and pour into a bowl. Pudding will thicken somewhat as it cools. Serve warm, or refrigerate and serve cold.

Cooking with Wild Rice

About Wild Rice

Wild rice is not truly rice, but rather an aquatic grass native to North America. Originally it grew wild in the rivers and lakes of the northern Great Lakes region, but it's now mostly cultivated in that area, as well as in Minnesota and California. Wild rice has a very distinctive, nutty flavor and is delicious when combined with brown or white rice, or with lentils and other legumes. Dried fruits are particularly complementary to wild rice. Look for long, slender, uniformly shaped grains for salads and side dishes. Less expensive broken grains can be used for soups or stuffings.

Basic Cooked Wild Rice
Makes 4 cups

Rinse the wild rice to remove any loose hulls. Cooking in chicken stock adds richness and flavor. Wild rice can also be cooked in orange, apple or tomato juice, particularly if it is going to be used in a salad. After draining, you can reserve the nutritious cooking liquid for soups or sauces.

3 cups water, chicken stock or other
   cooking liquid

½ tsp. salt
1 cup wild rice

In a large saucepan, bring water to a boil and add salt and rice. Reduce heat to low, cover and simmer for 40 to 45 minutes, until grains are tender and most have cracked open, exposing a fluffy white interior. Remove from heat and let stand covered for 10 minutes; drain if necessary.

Wild Rice Salad

A piquant mustard dressing adds punch to a melange of wild rice, glazed shallots, raisins and almonds. Serve this as an accompaniment to grilled duck breasts or Cornish game hens.

2-3 large shallots
1 tbs. butter
1 tbs. sherry vinegar
1 tbs. lemon juice
1 quarter-sized piece fresh ginger, peeled and finely minced
½ tsp. sugar
2 tsp. Dijon-style mustard

¼ cup olive oil
salt and freshly ground pepper to taste
3 cups *Basic Cooked Wild Rice*, page 74, cooled
⅓ cup slivered almonds or pine nuts, toasted
¼ cup golden raisins
2 tbs. chopped fresh parsley

Peel and trim shallots and cut into ¼-inch-thick slices widthwise. In a medium skillet, melt butter over medium heat and sauté shallots for 10 to 12 minutes, until tender and lightly browned. Remove from heat. In a small bowl, whisk together sherry vinegar, lemon juice, ginger, sugar and mustard. Slowly add olive oil, whisking until well blended. Season with salt and pepper. Place rice in a serving bowl and mix with dressing. Add sautéed shallots, almonds and raisins and toss lightly to combine. Stir in parsley and serve at room temperature.

Wild Rice Pancakes

Use leftover wild rice to make these savory pancakes. Serve them with roasted duck or any meat that is served with a rich sauce. These are great for brunch, too, when buttered and drizzled with a little maple syrup.

1 cup all-purpose flour
½ tsp. salt
1½ tsp. baking soda
3 tbs. butter
¼ cup thinly sliced green onions,
    white part only
2 large eggs

1¾ cups buttermilk
½ tsp. Worcestershire sauce
1 tsp. Dijon-style mustard
1½ cups *Basic Cooked Wild Rice*,
    page 74
2 tbs. chopped fresh parsley
freshly ground pepper to taste

In a small bowl, combine flour, salt and soda and stir well. In a small skillet, heat butter over medium heat and sauté onions for 2 to 3 minutes; remove from heat and cool. Heat griddle. In a medium bowl, whisk together eggs, buttermilk, Worcestershire and mustard. Add flour mixture and whisk until smooth. Add sautéed onion, wild rice, parsley and pepper and mix well. Spray griddle with non-stick vegetable spray or brush with oil. For each pancake, spoon about 3 tbs. rice mixture onto griddle and cook until done, turning once. Keep warm in a 200° oven until all pancakes have been made. Serve immediately.

Wild Rice Pepper Boats

Colorful peppers are stuffed with a savory wild rice, mushroom and cheese filling. Prepare the peppers early in the day and bake them just before serving.

4 large red or yellow bell peppers, cut in half lengthwise and seeded
2 tbs. full-flavored olive oil
1 cup finely chopped onion
8-10 cremini (brown) or shiitake mushrooms, coarsely chopped
2 cloves garlic, minced
leaves from 2 sprigs fresh thyme

pinch red pepper flakes
salt and freshly ground pepper to taste
½ cup chopped toasted walnuts
2 cups *Basic Cooked Wild Rice*, page 74
1 large egg, lightly beaten
¼ cup chopped sun-dried tomatoes
4 oz. feta cheese, crumbled, or 4 oz. smoked gouda, cut into ¼-inch cubes

Cook peppers in boiling water for 3 to 4 minutes, until peppers are softened, but still hold their shape; drain and cool. In a large skillet, heat oil over medium heat and sauté onion for 3 to 4 minutes. Add mushrooms and cook for 3 to 4 minutes, until they release their liquid. Add garlic, thyme, pepper flakes, salt and pepper; cook for 1 to 2 minutes. Cool for 5 to 10 minutes and stir in walnuts, wild rice, egg, tomatoes and cheese. Check seasonings. Heat oven to 350°. Divide filling among peppers and place in an oiled baking pan with about ⅓ cup water. Bake stuffed peppers uncovered for 20 to 25 minutes until hot. Serve warm.

Stir-Fried Chicken and Wild Rice in Lettuce Cups

For this dish, a hot chicken and wild rice filling is rolled up in crisp cold lettuce leaves, which are eaten out of hand like burritos. Serve these at an informal lunch or pair them with other salads or Asian dishes.

4 boneless, skinless chicken thighs (about 12 oz.), cut into ⅜-inch cubes
1 tbs. rice wine or dry sherry
1 tbs. soy sauce
1 tsp. toasted sesame oil
2 tbs. cornstarch
pinch white pepper
2 tbs. vegetable oil
1 tsp. minced fresh ginger
1 clove garlic, minced
2 tbs. minced green onions, white part only

¼ tsp. red pepper flakes, or to taste
2 tbs. hoisin sauce
⅓ cup *Basic Chicken Stock*, page 8, or canned chicken broth
2 tsp. apple cider vinegar
½ tsp. salt
2½ cups *Basic Cooked Wild Rice*, page 74
1 tbs. cold water
fresh cilantro leaves for garnish
large iceberg lettuce leaves for serving

Place chicken cubes in a small bowl with wine, soy sauce, sesame oil, 1 tbs. of the cornstarch and pepper; stir until well mixed. Let stand for 10 to 15 minutes.

Heat a wok or large skillet over medium heat. Add 2 tbs. vegetable oil. Add chicken mixture to wok and stir-fry for 2 to 3 minutes, until chicken is opaque. Add ginger, garlic, onions and pepper flakes and stir-fry for 1 to 2 minutes. Add hoisin sauce, chicken stock, vinegar and salt, stirring to mix. Add wild rice, reduce heat to low and cook for 3 to 4 minutes, stirring frequently. Combine remaining 1 tbs. cornstarch with 1 tbs. cold water and add to pan a little at a time, stirring until liquid thickens and forms a glaze. Pour mixture into a warm serving bowl and garnish with fresh cilantro leaves. Pass lettuce leaves and let diners fill their own leaves with chicken and wild rice filling.

Cooking with Corn

About Corn

Wild corn was domesticated by early residents of Central and South America long before the arrival of the Europeans. Corn was so important that most corn-growing tribes gave it almost god-like status, worshiping it in various ways. Native Americans taught European settlers to plant corn and it soon became a dietary staple.

Corn is versatile and can be incorporated into every meal and snack. Corn is a good source of carbohydrates and is high in B vitamins, potassium and magnesium.

Several common forms of corn are described below:

Cornmeal is made from dried, ground corn kernels. It comes in yellow, white or blue varieties, ground from yellow, white or blue corn kernels, respectively.

Polenta is a version of cornmeal made of both finely ground and coarsely ground cornmeal.

Corn flour is cornmeal that has been very finely ground. It is used in baking.

Grits are made from hominy, which is corn that has been soaked in wood ash or lye to loosen the outside hull and soften the kernel. There are many types of grits on the market today, some of which are made from untreated corn. Stone-ground grits have more flavor and texture than instant or quick-cooking grits. The most commonly available grits cook in about 5 minutes.

Basic Cooked Polenta

Starting the polenta in cold water helps to avoid lumps. Polenta doesn't need continuous attention, but should be stirred frequently to keep it from sticking to the bottom of your pot. For firm polenta, the mixture should be thick enough that a wooden spoon placed in the center will stand upright for 10 to 15 seconds.

4 cups cold water, *Basic Chicken Stock*,
   page 8, milk, or a combination
1 tsp. salt
1 cup coarse-ground polenta

2 tbs. butter, softened
freshly ground black pepper to taste
1/3 cup freshly grated Parmesan cheese
butter or olive oil, optional

In a large, heavy saucepan, add cold water and salt. Stir in polenta. Place over high heat and stir until water comes to a boil. Reduce heat to low and simmer for 10 to 15 minutes, stirring every few minutes. Cook until polenta is soft and creamy and grains are soft. Stir in butter, pepper and cheese. For soft polenta, serve immediately in a warmed large bowl or on a platter.

For firm polenta, transfer to a lightly oiled baking pan and spread to an even 9-x-9-x-1/2-inch square. Cover and refrigerate for at least 2 hours or overnight. Cut polenta into desired shapes, brush with melted butter or olive oil and reheat under the broiler or on a grill until golden brown. Or, sauté polenta shapes in a little butter until crisp and golden brown.

Cornmeal and Buttermilk Waffles

Makes eight 6-inch waffles

Crisp, flavorful and hearty, these cornmeal waffles can be mixed with a blender in less time than it takes to preheat the waffle iron. Bake the whole recipe and reheat the leftovers in the toaster for an easy breakfast on a busy morning. Or, serve hot waffles under creamed chicken or tuna for lunch or supper.

2 cups buttermilk
2 eggs
3 tbs. vegetable oil
1 tsp. salt
1 tbs. sugar
1¼ cups all-purpose flour
1 cup white, yellow or blue cornmeal
¼ tsp. Tabasco Jalapeño Sauce, optional
1 tsp. baking soda

Heat waffle iron. In a blender container, combine buttermilk, eggs, oil, salt, sugar, flour, cornmeal and Tabasco, if using, and process on high speed for 1 minute. Scrape down the sides of blender if necessary. Add baking soda and pulse 2 to 3 times to combine. Spray waffle grids with nonstick cooking spray. Bake waffles according to manufacturer's instructions for your waffle iron.

Baked Grits and Roasted Garlic Pudding

*This creamy pudding is perfect for brunch or as a side dish with roasted meat, duck or chicken. Try it topped with **Quick Tomato Sauce**, page 111, or your favorite fresh tomato salsa.*

4 cups milk
¼ tsp. dry mustard
1 tsp. salt
1 cup quick-cooking grits
3 tbs. butter

Roasted Garlic, page 159
¼ tsp. Tabasco Sauce
4 large eggs
½ cup freshly grated Parmesan cheese

Generously butter a 2-quart baking dish. Pour milk into a 3- to 4-quart saucepan and carefully bring just to a boil. Add mustard and salt. Slowly add grits to milk, stirring with a whisk. Reduce heat to low and simmer grits for 5 minutes, stirring frequently. Remove from heat and stir in butter, *Roasted Garlic* and Tabasco. Cool for at least 10 minutes. In a small bowl, whisk eggs until frothy and stir into grits mixture. Add cheese and mix well. Pour into baking dish and bake uncovered for 50 minutes. Serve immediately.

Southwestern Corn Cakes

These piquant fresh corn cakes make a delicious side dish for grilled fish or chicken. If using a super-sweet variety of corn, omit the sugar. Bake the cakes in nonstick muffin cups and time them to be done when the entrée is ready.

4 ears fresh white sweet corn, or 2
    cups frozen white corn kernels
1 cup corn flour
¼ tsp. salt
¼ tsp. baking powder
¼ tsp. dry mustard

2 tsp. sugar
2 large eggs
⅓ cup milk
1 jalapeño chile, stemmed, seeded
    and finely chopped
4 green onions, white part only, minced

Heat oven to 375°. With a sharp knife, cut down the center of each row of corn kernels; cut corn from ears and set aside. Generously butter an 8-cup muffin tin. In a small bowl, combine flour, salt, baking powder, mustard and sugar and stir well. In a medium bowl, whisk eggs with milk until frothy. Add flour mixture to egg mixture and whisk until smooth. Stir in corn, jalapeño and onions. Pour about ⅓ cup batter into each muffin cup. Bake for 20 to 25 minutes, until cakes are puffy and golden brown. Serve immediately.

Cornmeal Pizza Crust

This toasty cornmeal crust makes a delicious base for your favorite pizza topping. Be sure to use bread flour in this recipe to achieve the right texture. A preheated pizza stone produces a wonderful crisp crust. Or, you can bake it in a deep pizza pan lined with parchment paper. To make a pizza: Heat oven to 425°, spread the prebaked crust with your favorite topping and bake it for 12 to 15 minutes, until the topping is bubbling and the crust is golden.

1 cup warm water, about 105°
1½ cups bread flour
1 pkg. active-dry yeast

3 tbs. olive oil
1 cup cornmeal or polenta
½ tsp. salt

Place water in the bowl of a heavy-duty mixer and stir in ½ cup of the flour and yeast. Let stand for about 15 minutes, until bubbling. Stir in olive oil and cornmeal and let stand for 10 minutes. Attach dough hook and, with mixer running, add salt and remaining 1 cup flour. Mix on medium speed for 6 minutes. Dough will be quite soft. Place a sheet of parchment paper or aluminum foil on a work surface. Lightly oil hands and press dough into a 12-inch circle on parchment or foil. Crimp edges to make a slight ridge. Lightly cover with plastic wrap or foil and let crust rise for about 30 minutes.

Heat oven to 325°. Bake crust for about 20 minutes, until firm but not browned.

Taco-Style Cornmeal Pizza

Cooked taco filling with cheese and fresh salsa makes a zesty pizza. There will be a little taco meat left over that you can use as an omelet filling or in a quesadilla. Serve with a crisp green salad.

1 pkg. (1 oz.) taco seasoning mix
1 lb. lean ground beef
1 cup shredded mozzarella cheese
½ cup shredded sharp cheddar cheese
1 prebaked *Cornmeal Pizza Crust*, page 86
1 cup prepared mild or hot chunky salsa
fresh cilantro leaves for garnish

Heat oven to 425°. Follow directions on taco seasoning mix for cooking beef. There should be no liquid remaining in skillet after cooking. Sprinkle cheeses evenly over crust and top with a generous portion of seasoned beef. Top with salsa. Bake for 12 to 15 minutes, until hot and bubbling. Cut into wedges and serve immediately garnished with cilantro.

Salad-Topped Cornmeal Pizza

Servings: 4-6

A hot baked pizza crust topped with mixed greens, prosciutto and fresh figs or sliced pears makes a tempting first course or luncheon dish.

1 prebaked *Cornmeal Pizza Crust*, page 86
1 cup shredded mozzarella or fontina cheese
4 cups mixed baby salad greens, washed and dried
2 tsp. full-flavored olive oil
1 tsp. sherry vinegar
salt and freshly ground pepper to taste
4-6 fresh ripe figs, or 1 ripe pear
4 thin slices prosciutto or ham, cut into 2-inch squares
Parmesan cheese shavings for garnish

Heat oven to 400°. Sprinkle crust with cheese and bake for 10 minutes, until cheese melts. While crust is baking, toss salad greens in a medium bowl with oil, vinegar, salt and pepper. Trim figs and cut into quarters. If using a pear, peel, core and cut into thin slices. Remove crust from oven, cut into wedges and serve on plates. Distribute salad greens on wedges and top with figs or pear slices, prosciutto and a few Parmesan shavings. Serve immediately.

Sweet Polenta Cake

Serve this treat with a little raspberry or strawberry sauce, or accompanied by some fresh berries.

½ cup golden raisins
2 tbs. orange liqueur or orange juice
½ cup uncooked polenta
1½ cups milk
⅛ tsp. salt
⅓ cup plus 1 tbs. sugar

2 tbs. butter, room temperature
3 large eggs, lightly beaten
1 tsp. vanilla extract
generous amount freshly grated
  nutmeg
¼ cup pine nuts

Heat oven to 375°. In a small bowl, combine raisins and orange liqueur; set aside. Oil an 8-x-8-inch baking pan and line bottom with parchment.

In a deep 2-quart microwavable bowl, combine polenta, milk and salt. Cover and microwave on HIGH for 5 minutes; stir mixture. Return bowl to microwave and cook on HIGH for 5 minutes. Transfer mixture to a large bowl and whisk in ⅓ cup sugar and butter until smooth. Cool for 5 minutes. Add eggs, raisins and liqueur, vanilla and nutmeg and stir lightly. Pour batter into prepared pan and sprinkle evenly with pine nuts and remaining 1 tbs. sugar. Bake for about 35 to 40 minutes, until cake is lightly browned and puffy. Cool to room temperature. Cut into squares to serve.

Cooking with Oats

About Oats

Oats have been cultivated since about the time of Christ. Oats, especially the bran, have recently received attention for their cholesterol-reducing properties. Oats have significant quantities of fiber, protein and trace minerals. Unlike many other grains, the oat germ, which contains oil, is not removed during processing; therefore, oats have a higher fat content than many other grains.

Oats are available in many forms; some examples follow:

Rolled oats, also called old-fashioned oats, are made by slicing raw oats before steaming and "rolling" them into flakes.

Steel-cut oats, or Irish or Scotch oats, are whole-grain oats that have been coarsely sliced with sharp steel blades, which lends a chewy texture.

Quick-cooking oats are processed the same way as rolled oats, but they are rolled into very thin slices over a hot surface, which precooks them slightly.

Oat flour is made from finely ground oat groats. It has no gluten, so it must be used in conjunction with wheat flour in baking. In general, you can replace up to 25% of the wheat flour with oat flour in yeast breads and, depending on the recipe, up to 100% of the wheat flour in other baking recipes. Using oat flour lends a creamy, soft and moist texture to baked goods.

Hot Apple and Steel-Cut Oats Breakfast

Servings: 6

Steel-cut oats have a chewier texture and more flavor than traditional rolled oats. Make this dish with apples or another favorite dried fruit before you go to bed. At breakfast time, spoon the mixture into a bowl and microwave it for a quick, nutritious breakfast. This can be refrigerated for up to a week.

2 cups apple juice
2 cups water
1 cup Irish steel-cut oats
¾ cup diced dried apples, apricots,
   peaches or a mixture
1 tbs. brown sugar, plus more
   for serving, optional

1 tbs. butter, optional
¼ tsp. cinnamon
dash freshly grated nutmeg
¼ tsp. salt
1 tbs. lemon juice
milk for serving

In a medium saucepan, bring juice and water to a boil over high heat. Stir in oats, apples, brown sugar, butter, if using, cinnamon, nutmeg and salt. Reduce heat to low and simmer uncovered for 30 minutes. Add lemon juice, ladle into cereal bowls and serve with milk and more sugar, if desired.

If making ahead, pour mixture into a covered container and refrigerate until ready to serve. Reheat in the microwave.

Apple and Oat Waffles

Oat flour, rolled oats and grated apple give an interesting texture to these fragrant waffles.

1½ cups oat flour
¼ cup regular rolled oats
1 tsp. cinnamon
2 tsp. baking powder
½ tsp. salt
2 large eggs

2 tbs. honey
1¼ cups milk
1 tsp. vanilla extract
1 medium Golden Delicious or Granny
    Smith apple, peeled and grated
3 tbs. butter, melted

Heat waffle iron. In a large bowl, stir together oat flour, rolled oats, cinnamon, baking powder and salt. In another bowl, whisk eggs until frothy and beat in honey, milk and vanilla. Pour egg mixture into flour mixture and stir just to combine. Fold in grated apple and melted butter. Spray waffle grids with nonstick cooking spray. Bake waffles according to manufacturer's instructions for your waffle iron.

Banana Pecan Bread

Make this not-too-sweet bread when you have very ripe, soft bananas on hand. It tastes even better on the second day and is delicious toasted.

¼ cup butter, softened
1 cup sugar
2 eggs
1 cup mashed very ripe bananas (about 2 medium)
2 cups oat flour
1 tsp. baking soda
½ tsp. salt
⅓ cup buttermilk
½ cup chopped pecans

Heat oven to 350°. Oil a 9-x-5-inch loaf pan. With a mixer, beat butter and sugar until light and fluffy. Add eggs and bananas and mix well. In a small bowl, combine flour, baking soda and salt and mix well. With mixer on low speed, mix flour mixture into egg mixture alternately with buttermilk. Continue mixing just until dry ingredients are combined. Fold in pecans. Spoon batter into prepared pan and bake for about 1 hour and 10 minutes, or until a toothpick inserted into the center comes out clean. Cool on a rack.

Sugar and Spice Muffins

Mix up this muffin batter in the time it takes the oven to heat. Dip the baked muffins into cinnamon-sugar while still warm and watch them disappear.

½ cup butter, softened
1 cup sugar
1 egg
½ cup oat flour
1 cup all-purpose flour
2 tsp. baking powder

½ tsp. salt
¼ tsp. nutmeg
½ cup milk
1 tsp. cinnamon
⅓ cup butter, melted

Heat oven to 350°. Butter a 12-cup muffin tin. With a mixer, beat ½ cup butter and ½ cup of the sugar until light and fluffy. Add egg and mix well. In a small bowl, mix together flours, baking powder, salt and nutmeg. Gradually add flour mixture to butter mixture alternately with milk, mixing well after each addition. Distribute batter evenly in muffin cups. Bake for 20 to 25 minutes, until lightly browned and firm to the touch.

While muffins are baking, mix remaining ½ cup sugar with cinnamon. Remove hot muffins from pan. Dip top of each muffin into melted butter and then into sugar-cinnamon mixture. Serve immediately.

Oat-Corn Crackers with
Black Bean-Cilantro Pesto Dip

Makes 60-80

These hearty, aromatic crackers are also a nice accompaniment for a cheese plate. Store the crackers in an airtight container.

1¼ cups bread flour
1 cup corn flour
2 tsp. baking powder
1 tsp. baking soda
½ tsp. dry mustard
1 tsp. salt

1 tbs. sugar
1 cup regular rolled oats
1 cup buttermilk
3 tbs. butter, softened
Black Bean-Cilantro Pesto Dip,
  follows

Heat oven to 400°. In a bowl, combine flours, baking powder, soda, mustard, salt and sugar; mix well. With a food processor, process oats and buttermilk for 20 seconds. Add butter and pulse until mixed. Add flour mixture and process for 30 seconds. Transfer dough to a floured work surface and knead by hand for 1 to 2 minutes (dough will be quite soft and sticky). Divide dough into 3 equal pieces and form each piece into a 4-x-6-inch rectangle. Let dough rest for 10 minutes. Roll each piece into a rectangle about ¹⁄₁₆-inch thick and place on a parchment-lined baking sheet. With a pastry wheel or pizza cutter, cut each rectangle into 3-inch squares and cut each square diagonally into triangles. Bake for 12 to 15 minutes.

If crackers aren't totally crisp, reduce oven heat to 250° and bake for a few more minutes. Cool on a rack. Serve with *Black Bean-Cilantro Pesto Dip*.

Black Bean-Cilantro Pesto Dip

*If you have some **Cilantro Pesto**, page 31, already on hand, this dip goes together quickly. Tortilla or corn chips also make delicious dippers.*

1 can (15 oz.) black beans
¼ cup *Cilantro Pesto*, page 31
1 large ripe tomato, peeled, seeded and coarsely chopped
paprika
fresh cilantro leaves for garnish

Drain beans, rinse well under cold water and drain again. Place beans in a food processor workbowl with *Cilantro Pesto* and process until fairly smooth. Scrape down the sides of bowl. Add tomato and pulse 2 to 3 times, leaving small chunks of tomato visible in mixture. Spoon dip into a serving bowl, sprinkle with paprika and garnish with fresh cilantro leaves.

Dried Cherry Cake

Oat flour, rolled oats and dried cherries make a delicious cake for breakfast or dessert. Substitute dried cranberries or blueberries for cherries if you like.

¼ cup brown sugar, packed
½ cup plus 2 tbs. oat flour
½ tsp. salt
¼ tsp. cinnamon
¼ tsp. nutmeg
5 tbs. butter
½ cup regular rolled oats
½ cup all-purpose flour
¼ cup granulated sugar
1 tsp. baking powder
1 egg, lightly beaten
⅓ cup milk
grated peel (zest) of 1 lemon
¾ cup dried cherries

Heat oven to 350°. Butter an 8-x-8-inch baking pan. In a food processor work-bowl, combine brown sugar, 2 tbs. oat flour, 1/4 tsp. of the salt, cinnamon and nutmeg. Add 2 tbs. of the butter and pulse 6 to 8 times, until mixture resembles coarse meal. Transfer mixture to a small bowl, stir in oats and set aside.

In food processor workbowl, combine 1/2 cup oat flour, all-purpose flour, granulated sugar, baking powder and remaining 1/4 tsp. salt. Add remaining 3 tbs. butter and pulse 6 to 8 times, until mixture resembles coarse meal. Add egg, milk and lemon zest and pulse 4 to 5 times, just until dry ingredients are moistened. Remove blade from workbowl and stir in cherries. Batter will be sticky. Spoon batter into prepared baking pan and sprinkle oat mixture evenly over the top. Bake for 40 to 45 minutes, until topping is lightly browned and a toothpick inserted into the center comes out clean. Serve warm or at room temperature.

Plum Crisp with Oatmeal-Walnut Topping

This is the perfect finish for a summer dinner served warm or at room temperature. Top the crisp with a little whipped cream or vanilla ice cream if you like. Sliced peaches or nectarines can be substituted for the plums.

2 lb. fresh plums
¼ cup granulated sugar
grated peel (zest) of 1 lemon
1 tbs. lemon juice
¼ tsp. salt
½ cup brown sugar, packed

1 tsp. cinnamon
½ cup oat flour or all-purpose flour
½ cup cold butter, cut into 12 pieces
½ cup regular rolled oats
½ cup chopped toasted walnuts

Heat oven to 350°. Cut plums in half, remove and discard pits and cut fruit into ½-inch slices. Place fruit in a buttered 8-x-10-inch baking dish. Add granulated sugar, lemon zest, lemon juice and ⅛ tsp. of the salt and toss lightly to mix.

In a food processor workbowl, combine brown sugar, cinnamon, oat flour and remaining ⅛ tsp. salt and pulse 1 to 2 times. Add butter and pulse until butter mixture is the size of small peas. Transfer mixture to a bowl and stir in oats and walnuts. Distribute oat mixture evenly over fruit. Bake for 40 to 45 minutes, until fruit is bubbling and topping is nicely browned and crisp.

Cooking with Millet

About Millet

Before written history, millet was widely grown in India, China and North Africa. Like barley, millet steadily declined in importance in many cultures as wheat and rice became more available. Although most consumers primarily think of it as a component of bird seed, cooked millet is delicious.

Millet is gluten-free, which makes it a good grain for people who are allergic to wheat. Millet is also rich in fiber and protein. Millet cooks in about the same time as white rice and can be substituted for it in many rice recipes. Try millet in soups, salads and main courses.

Some popular forms of millet are listed below:

Hulled millet seeds are whole-grain millet from which the indigestible outer hull has been removed.

Millet flour is made from ground millet seeds. It has a slightly sweet flavor. Up to 10% of the wheat flour in bread recipes can be replaced by millet flour.

Puffed millet is a popular breakfast cereal and can be used for a crunchy topping for baked goods. It is similar to puffed rice and puffed wheat. Look for it in boxes in the cereal aisle of the supermarket or in bulk bins.

Basic Cooked Millet

Hulled millet is more flavorful when it is toasted before cooking.

¾ cup hulled millet seeds
2 cups water or stock
¼ tsp. salt

To toast millet, place in a heavy skillet and cook over medium-high heat, stirring constantly, for 4 to 5 minutes, or until millet is lightly browned and has a toasty aroma. Remove from heat.

To cook millet, pour toasted millet into a large saucepan. Add water and salt and bring to a boil over high heat. Cover pan, reduce heat to low and simmer for about 20 minutes, until most of the water has been absorbed. Remove from heat and let stand for 10 minutes. Remove lid and fluff grains with a fork. Cool to room temperature before refrigerating. Keeps covered for 2 to 3 days in the refrigerator.

Tuna Millet Salad

This salad travels well and makes great lunchbox or picnic fare. Roll it up in lettuce leaves or spoon it into radicchio cups for an attractive presentation. This recipe doubles easily.

1 cup *Basic Cooked Millet*, page 103
1 can (6½ oz.) water- or oil-packed tuna*, drained
⅓ cup finely chopped celery
1 medium tomato, peeled, seeded and chopped (about ½ cup)
2 tbs. finely chopped green onions or fresh chives

¼ cup chopped fresh parsley
¼ tsp. Tabasco Jalapeño Sauce
salt and freshly ground pepper to taste
2 tbs. buttermilk
1 tbs. lemon juice
2 tsp. full-flavored olive oil
butter lettuce or radicchio leaves, optional

In a medium bowl, combine millet, tuna, celery, tomato, onions and parsley and lightly toss together. Stir in Tabasco, salt and pepper. Stir in buttermilk, lemon juice and olive oil. Adjust seasonings. Serve immediately spooned into lettuce or radicchio leaves, if desired. Refrigerate for up to 2 days. Bring to room temperature before serving.

***Note**: If using oil-packed tuna, reduce olive oil to 1 teaspoon.

Curried Lentils and Millet

This savory vegetarian side dish is satisfying for lunch or supper when accompanied by a green salad. Or, serve it with roasted chicken or pork. Check lentils for stones or other materials that may have slipped through during processing.

3 tbs. vegetable oil
1 large yellow onion, chopped
1 small carrot, coarsely grated
1 jalapeño chile, stemmed, seeded
    and finely minced
1 tbs. curry powder
½ cup toasted millet (see page 103)
1 cup brown lentils, rinsed

3½ cups *Basic Vegetable Stock*, page
    10, or canned vegetable broth
salt and freshly ground pepper to taste
hot pepper sauce to taste, optional
¼ cup chopped fresh cilantro
¼ cup chopped fresh mint
plain yogurt for garnish, optional

In a heavy 3½- to 4-quart pot, heat oil over medium-low heat. Add onion and sauté for 5 to 7 minutes, until soft and translucent. Add carrot, jalapeño and curry powder and sauté for 1 minute, or until curry powder is fragrant. Add millet and stir to coat well. Add lentils and stock and bring to a boil over high heat. Partially cover pot, reduce heat to low and simmer for 35 to 45 minutes, until lentils are tender. Stir in salt, pepper and hot pepper sauce. Sprinkle with cilantro and mint and top with dollops of yogurt, if desired. Serve hot.

Millet-Stuffed Artichokes

Use a grapefruit spoon or melon baller to scrape out each prickly "choke" before filling the artichokes with this savory herb stuffing.

juice of 1 lemon
4 medium artichokes (about 8 oz. each)
3 tbs. full-flavored olive oil
1 cup fresh breadcrumbs
2 cloves garlic, finely chopped
1 cup *Basic Cooked Millet*, page 103
1 tbs. finely chopped fresh parsley
1 tbs. finely chopped fresh mint
2 tbs. white wine vinegar or lemon juice
2 tbs. pine nuts, toasted
1/4 cup freshly grated Parmesan cheese
salt and freshly ground pepper to taste

Fill a large bowl with cold water and add lemon juice. Wash artichokes and cut stems flush with bottoms to make flat bases. With a large knife, cut straight across the top of artichokes about 1 inch down. Remove 2 or 3 layers of outer leaves and trim rough edges of artichoke bottom where leaves were removed.

Gently spread artichoke leaves and, using a sharp spoon or melon baller, remove prickly center leaves. Scrape out as much of the fuzzy choke as possible and discard. Immediately place trimmed artichokes in lemon water.

In a large skillet, heat 2 tbs. of the olive oil over medium heat. Add breadcrumbs and sauté until lightly browned and crisp. Add garlic and sauté for 30 seconds; remove from heat. Transfer breadcrumb mixture to a medium bowl. Add millet, parsley, mint, vinegar, pine nuts, Parmesan cheese, salt and pepper and mix well.

Drain artichokes up-side down on paper towels for 2 to 3 minutes. Push stuffing to one side of bowl and place 1 artichoke in bowl with stuffing. Using about ¼ of the stuffing for each artichoke, spoon some filling into the center of artichoke. Gently spread leaves and spoon a little stuffing between them. It isn't necessary to put filling beside every leaf; do not pack stuffing tightly. Repeat with remaining artichokes and filling.

As artichokes are stuffed, place them in a pot with a tight-fitting lid just large enough to hold them. To pot, add water to a depth of 1 inch. Drizzle remaining 1 tbs. olive oil over artichokes. Cover pot and bring water just to a boil over high heat. Immediately reduce heat to low and simmer for 40 to 45 minutes, until each artichoke base is tender when pierced with a knife. Check occasionally to see if additional water is needed. Serve warm or at room temperature.

Black Bean Enchiladas
with Red Pepper Sauce

Makes 8-10

To soften corn tortillas, hold them with kitchen tongs over a low flame or a medium-hot electric burner for a few seconds. Turn tortillas over several times until they become pliable.

1 can (15 oz.) black beans, rinsed and drained
1½ cups *Basic Cooked Millet*, page 103
1 can (4 oz.) chopped green chiles
2 cups coarsely shredded Monterey Jack or cheddar cheese
salt and freshly ground pepper to taste
1 tbs. vegetable oil
⅓ cup finely chopped onion
1¾ cups *Basic Chicken Stock*, page 8, or canned chicken broth
2 medium roasted red bell peppers, about 1 cup
3 tbs. tomato paste
2 tsp. chili powder
4-5 drops Tabasco Sauce, or to taste
8-10 corn tortillas

In a bowl, combine black beans, millet, chiles and 1 cup of the cheese; mix well and season with salt and pepper. In a medium skillet, heat oil over medium heat and sauté onion for 3 to 4 minutes, until soft. In a blender container or food processor workbowl, combine sautéed onion, stock, red peppers and tomato paste and process until smooth. Transfer mixture to skillet with chili powder and Tabasco. Heat mixture over medium-high heat for 8 to 10 minutes, until slightly reduced and thickened. Pour ½ of the sauce into bowl with bean-millet mixture.

Heat oven to 375°. Lightly oil a 9-x-13-inch pan. Soften corn tortillas and dip both sides in sauce in skillet. Spoon about ¼ cup filling down the center of tortilla and roll up cigar-fashion. Place filled tortilla seam-side down in prepared pan and repeat rolling process with remaining tortillas and filling. Pour remaining sauce evenly over filled tortillas and sprinkle with remaining 1 cup cheese. Bake for 12 to 15 minutes, until enchiladas are heated through and cheese is melted. Serve hot.

Sausage-Stuffed Asian Eggplants

Serve a plate of small garden eggplants stuffed with a zesty sausage filling for a summer supper or patio luncheon. Hollowed-out zucchini, yellow squash, red or yellow bell peppers and tomato halves also work well with this stuffing. Small red or yellow bell peppers will bake in 35 to 40 minutes. Tomatoes or zucchini will take about 25 minutes.

4 Japanese or Chinese eggplants
  (about 4 oz. each)
1-2 tsp. salt
½ lb. mild Italian-style sausage,
  casings removed
½ cup finely chopped onion
3 cloves garlic, finely chopped
¼ tsp. red pepper flakes

1 tbs. tomato paste
½ cup *Basic Cooked Millet*, page 103
2 tbs. finely chopped fresh parsley
½ tsp. fresh thyme leaves
salt and freshly ground pepper to taste
¼ cup freshly grated Parmesan cheese
Quick Tomato Sauce, follows, optional

Trim eggplants and cut in half lengthwise. With a small sharp knife, cut around edge of eggplants leaving a ¼-inch shell. Scoop out center pulp. Remove as many seeds as possible and coarsely chop eggplant pulp. Bring a large pot of water to a boil and add salt. Cook eggplant shells in boiling water for 1 minute; remove and drain (cut-side down) on paper towels. Add eggplant pulp to pot and cook for 1 minute; drain and set aside.

Crumble sausage into a medium skillet and sauté over medium heat for 5 to 6 minutes, until no longer pink, breaking it up with a spatula. To skillet, add onion, garlic and eggplant pulp and sauté for 8 to 10 minutes, until vegetables are soft and sausage is lightly browned. Remove from heat, add pepper flakes, tomato paste, millet, parsley, thyme, salt, pepper and Parmesan and mix well. Heat oven to 350°. Lightly oil a baking pan large enough to hold eggplants. Pour about ½ inch water into pan. Fill eggplant shells with stuffing and place in pan. Bake for 25 to 30 minutes, until eggplant shells are soft, but not collapsing, and filling is nicely browned. Serve warm or at room temperature with tomato sauce, if desired.

Quick Tomato Sauce

Makes about 2 cups

This bright-flavored sauce can be served hot or cold.

1 can (14 oz.) ready-cut tomatoes
1 tsp. full-flavored olive oil
1 tbs. red or white wine vinegar
1 tbs. balsamic vinegar
⅛ tsp. ground anise, optional

5-6 drops Tabasco Sauce
1 tsp. dried sweet basil, or 1 tbs. finely
   chopped fresh
salt and freshly ground pepper to taste

With a food processor, puree tomatoes until smooth. Transfer tomatoes to a small saucepan with remaining ingredients and bring to a boil over medium-high heat. Reduce heat to medium-low and simmer for 1 to 2 minutes.

Spinach-Millet Gnocchi

*These make a tasty first course accompanied by **Quick Tomato Sauce**, page 111. Or, serve them without tomato sauce as a side dish to accompany a roast. Allow time for the gnocchi mixture to chill in the refrigerator before cooking.*

¼ cup butter
¼ cup minced shallots or onion
1 large clove garlic, finely chopped
1 pkg. (10 oz.) frozen chopped spinach, thawed and squeezed very dry
1 cup *Basic Cooked Millet*, page 103
⅓ cup ricotta cheese
1 large egg, lightly beaten
⅓ cup flour
⅓ cup freshly grated Parmesan cheese
pinch nutmeg
salt and freshly ground pepper to taste
1 tbs. salt
hot *Quick Tomato Sauce*, page 111

In a medium skillet, melt 2 tbs. of the butter over medium-low heat. Add shallots and sauté for 2 to 3 minutes; add garlic and sauté for 1 minute. Add spinach and millet and sauté for 4 to 5 minutes, until moisture has evaporated and mixture is dry. Remove skillet from heat, transfer spinach mixture to a bowl and cool for 10 minutes. To bowl, add ricotta, egg, flour, ¼ cup of the Parmesan, nutmeg, salt and pepper and mix well. Cover mixture and refrigerate until very firm, about 1 hour.

In a large shallow saucepan, bring about 2½ quarts water to a boil over high heat. Add 1 tbs. salt and reduce heat to low. Shape gnocchi mixture into small balls about 1½ inches in diameter. Gently drop gnocchi into simmering water, 8 to 10 at a time, and cook for 7 to 8 minutes, until gnocchi float and are slightly firm to the touch. Carefully remove gnocchi with a slotted spoon and drain on paper towels. If some have ragged edges or fall apart, gently reshape when cool enough to handle.

Heat broiler. In an ovenproof skillet or serving dish, melt 1 tbs. of the butter. Place gnocchi close together in pan, drizzle with remaining 1 tbs. butter and sprinkle with remaining Parmesan cheese. Place pan under broiler about 3 to 4 inches from heat source for 2 to 3 minutes, until cheese is melted and lightly browned. Spoon a small amount of *Quick Tomato Sauce* on warm serving plates, top with a few gnocchi and serve immediately.

Apple-Cranberry Crisp
with Puffed Millet Topping

This is a terrific fall or winter dessert. Cook the apples first and cool them before adding the topping. Serve the crisp with a dollop of vanilla or cinnamon ice cream.

2½ lb. Granny Smith or other tart cooking apples (about 5)
1 tbs. lemon juice
2 tbs. butter
¼ cup granulated sugar
1 tbs. brandy or rum
¼ cup dried cranberries or golden raisins
grated peel (zest) from 1 lemon
¼ cup all-purpose flour
⅓ cup brown sugar, packed
½ tsp. cinnamon
5 tbs. butter, cut into pieces
¾ cup puffed millet

Peel, core and slice apples about ⅓-inch thick. Place apples in a bowl and toss with lemon juice. In a large skillet, heat 2 tbs. butter over high heat until foaming. Add apples and sauté for about 5 minutes, until starting to soften. To skillet, add sugar, brandy, cranberries and lemon zest and continue to cook for about 5 minutes, until apples are tender. Remove from heat and cool to room temperature.

In the workbowl of a food processor, combine flour, brown sugar, cinnamon and 5 tbs. butter and process until butter pieces are the size of small peas. Transfer mixture to a bowl with puffed millet, stirring until well mixed. Refrigerate until ready to bake.

Heat oven to 375°. Generously butter an 8-x-8-inch baking pan and add cooled apples. Sprinkle puffed millet mixture evenly over apples. Bake for 25 to 30 minutes, until apples are warmed through and topping is brown and crisp. Serve warm or at room temperature.

Puffed Millet, Walnut and Raisin Chews

For these sweet cookie bars, a prebaked pastry crust is spread with a nut, raisin and millet topping.

¼ cup butter
1½ cups brown sugar, packed
½ cup all-purpose flour
½ cup millet flour
pinch salt
2 large eggs
¼ tsp. salt
grated peel (zest) of 1 orange, or ¼ tsp. orange extract
1 tsp. vanilla extract
1 cup chopped walnuts
½ cup golden or dark raisins
1½ cups puffed millet

Heat oven to 350°. Lightly oil a 9-x-9-inch baking pan. In the workbowl of a food processor, combine butter, ½ cup of the sugar, flours and pinch salt and pulse several times, until mixture resembles coarse meal. Transfer mixture to prepared baking pan, pressing mixture down firmly and evenly over bottom of pan. Bake for 15 minutes, until lightly browned. Cool on a rack.

With a mixer, beat eggs with remaining 1 cup sugar until light and fluffy. Add salt, orange zest and vanilla and mix well. Stir in nuts, raisins and millet. Pour millet mixture over baked crust and spread evenly to pan edges. Bake for about 30 minutes, until topping is firm and golden brown. Cool on rack. Cut into squares while still warm.

Cooking with Buckwheat

About Buckwheat

Buckwheat is not a true grain, but is treated as such in cooking. Buckwheat is related to the rhubarb family and probably originated in Asia, where it has been grown for at least a thousand years. Buckwheat was introduced into Europe in the Middle Ages and became an important food resource in Russia, northern Italy and parts of France.

Buckwheat is high in protein, potassium and phosphorus and has a distinctive, somewhat earthy taste. It is versatile and comes in many forms.

Some common forms of buckwheat follow:

Kasha is the familiar name for roasted buckwheat goats or kernels. Kasha is a quick-cooking grain that can be cooked in milk for a nutritious hot breakfast cereal, or cooked in water or stock for pilafs or salads.

Buckwheat flour, made from ground buckwheat seeds, has a pronounced flavor. Buckwheat flour is most often used in blinis (tiny Russian-style savory pancakes) and breakfast pancakes.

Soba are Japanese-style noodles made from buckwheat and wheat flour. Soba can be used in much the same way as wheat pasta.

Basic Cooked Kasha (Roasted Buckwheat Groats)

*There are two kinds of kasha: a lightly roasted type and a darker roasted version, with a more assertive flavor. Coating the kasha with egg before cooking produces individual grains after cooking. Cooking kasha in broth adds flavor and is suggested for **Kasha Mushroom Paté**, page 122, and **Kasha Potato Salad**, page 125.*

2 cups water or stock
salt (if not using canned broth)
1 large egg, lightly beaten
1 cup kasha

In a large saucepan, bring water to a boil. Add salt, if using. In a bowl, combine egg and kasha and stir to thoroughly coat kasha with egg. Heat a heavy nonstick skillet over medium heat and stir-fry kasha for 3 to 4 minutes, until kasha grains separate, stirring to break up any clumps. Immediately pour kasha grains into boiling water, cover, reduce heat to low and simmer for 8 to 10 minutes, until kasha is tender. Remove kasha from heat and drain, if necessary. Fluff grains with a fork and cool.

Buckwheat Corn Pancakes

Tender and flavorful, these pancakes go together quickly and are delicious smothered in maple syrup. Or, make miniature pancakes and serve them with smoked salmon and sour cream to accompany champagne. Baked pancakes will keep for several days in the refrigerator or longer in the freezer. To serve, place on serving plate, drizzle with a little syrup, cover and reheat briefly in the microwave.

2 cups buttermilk
2 large eggs
¼ cup canola oil
¾ tsp. salt
½ cup buckwheat flour

½ cup corn flour
½ cup all-purpose flour
2 tsp. baking soda
maple syrup or honey for serving

In a bowl, combine buttermilk, eggs, oil and salt and whisk until well blended. In another bowl, stir together flours and baking soda. Add flour mixture to buttermilk mixture and whisk until just combined.

Heat a griddle or large skillet over medium heat. When hot, wipe skillet with an oil-saturated paper towel. For each pancake, spoon about 3 tbs. of the batter on griddle. When large holes form in batter, flip pancakes with a spatula. Cook pancakes briefly on second side. Serve on warm plates with maple syrup or honey.

Kasha-Mushroom Paté with Yogurt Sauce

Serve this as a first course with a small mixed baby green salad. Or, serve slices of it in sandwiches with lots of mustard. Use a food processor to quickly chop the mushrooms. Serve the tangy yogurt sauce on the side or spoon a ribbon of sauce over slices on a platter.

½ oz. dried porcini or shiitake
   mushrooms
1 cup hot water
1¼ cups *Basic Chicken Stock*, page 8,
   or canned chicken broth
½ cup uncooked kasha
1 carrot, peeled and cut into ½-inch dice
2 tbs. full-flavored olive oil
1 large onion, chopped
½ lb. fresh cremini (brown) mushrooms,
   trimmed and finely chopped
2 cloves garlic, finely chopped

2 tbs. brandy, optional
salt and black pepper to taste
2 large eggs
½ tsp. ground allspice
2 tsp. chopped fresh tarragon, or
   1 tsp. dried
2 tbs. chopped fresh parsley
2 tsp. Dijon-style mustard
1 tbs. tomato paste
3-4 drops Tabasco Sauce
3 tbs. dried breadcrumbs
Yogurt Sauce, follows

Place dried mushrooms in a small bowl with hot water and let stand for about 20 minutes, until soft. Drain and chop coarsely. Strain mushroom liquid and reserve for another use, if desired.

In a medium saucepan, bring chicken stock to a boil over high heat. Add kasha and carrot pieces. Cover pan, reduce heat to low and simmer covered for 8 to 10 minutes, until carrot is tender. Remove from heat and let stand covered for 5 minutes. Remove lid and fluff grains with a fork. In a large skillet, heat olive oil over medium heat and sauté onion for 5 to 6 minutes. Add fresh mushrooms, garlic, brandy, salt and pepper and cook for 4 to 5 minutes, until mushroom mixture is very dry. Remove from heat and cool for 10 minutes, stirring once or twice.

Heat oven to 350°. Oil a 6-cup loaf pan. Cut a strip of parchment paper or aluminum foil wide enough to cover the bottom of pan with edges extending up the sides. In a large bowl, whisk eggs. Add allspice, tarragon, parsley, mustard, tomato paste, Tabasco, salt and pepper. Stir in chopped dried mushrooms, kasha mixture and carrots. Add cooled mushroom mixture and breadcrumbs and mix well. Spread mixture in prepared pan. Bake uncovered for 1 hour or until paté is firm and lightly browned. Remove from oven, cool on a rack and refrigerate for several hours before serving. Cut into ½- to ¾-inch slices and serve with *Yogurt Sauce*.

Yogurt Sauce
Makes about 1 cup

⅔ cup plain yogurt
2 tbs. Dijon-style mustard

1 tbs. sugar
pinch white pepper

Whisk ingredients together in a small bowl. Refrigerate until ready to serve.

Kasha-Carrot Salad with Mustard Dressing

Cooking the diced carrots ahead of time makes this a quick salad to put together. This salad can be refrigerated for several hours, but bring it to room temperature before serving.

2 cups cooled *Basic Cooked Kasha*,
   page 120
2 cups diced cooked carrots, ⅜-inch
   dice
salt and freshly ground pepper to taste
3 tbs. olive oil
1 tbs. rice vinegar
2 tbs. lemon juice

4 tsp. Dijon-style mustard
½ tsp. sugar
1 tsp. sesame oil
½ tsp. grated fresh ginger
red pepper flakes to taste
¼ cup fresh cilantro leaves, packed
2 tbs. chopped fresh parsley

In a medium bowl, combine kasha and carrots. Season with salt and pepper and mix well. In a blender container or food processor workbowl, combine olive oil, vinegar, lemon juice, mustard, sugar, sesame oil, ginger, pepper flakes and cilantro leaves. Process until mixture is creamy. Pour dressing over kasha mixture and mix well. Check seasonings. Add chopped parsley and toss well.

Kasha-Potato Salad

Kasha adds protein and a delicious nutty aroma to this potato salad. Cook the kasha in chicken stock for added flavor.

1 lb. small red potatoes
1 cup *Basic Cooked Kasha*, page 120
¼ cup finely diced white onion
2 tbs. capers, rinsed and drained
salt and freshly ground pepper to taste
¼ cup sour cream or yogurt
¼ cup mayonnaise
2 tbs. Dijon-style mustard
1 tbs. milk

Cook potatoes in boiling water for about 20 minutes, until just tender. Drain and let stand for a few minutes until cool enough to peel. With a paring knife, remove peels from potatoes, cut into ½-inch pieces and place in a large bowl. To bowl, add cooked kasha, onion, capers, salt and pepper. In a small bowl, whisk together sour cream, mayonnaise, mustard, milk, salt and pepper. Pour sour cream mixture over potato mixture and stir gently until mixed. Refrigerate until ready to serve, for up to 2 days.

Cold Soba Noodle Salad

Serve this colorful Asian-style salad as the main attraction for a light lunch. Or, serve it as an appetizing addition to a picnic or buffet.

5 dried shiitake mushrooms
1 cup hot water
4 oz. snow peas (about 15)
¼ red or green bell pepper, cut into thin strips
5 green onions, white part only, thinly sliced
½ cup coarsely grated carrot
6 oz. soba noodles
1 tbs. salt
1 tbs. Dijon-style mustard
1 tbs. soy sauce or tamari
2 tbs. rice vinegar
1 tsp. grated fresh ginger
1 tbs. vegetable oil
1 tsp. toasted sesame oil
salt and white pepper to taste

Place mushrooms in a small bowl, cover with hot water and let stand for 20 minutes, until softened. Drain mushrooms, remove and discard stems and cut mushrooms into thin strips. Cook snow peas in boiling water for 30 seconds. Drain snow peas and cut lengthwise into thin strips.

Bring a large pot of water to a boil. Add salt and stir in noodles. Cook noodles according to package directions, until cooked through, but still slightly firm to the bite (*al dente*).

While noodles are cooking, combine mustard, soy sauce, vinegar and grated ginger in a large salad bowl. Slowly add vegetable and sesame oils, whisking until dressing thickens.

Drain cooked noodles well and pour into bowl with dressing. Toss to coat noodles with dressing and season with salt and pepper. Add mushrooms and vegetables and toss again. Serve at room temperature.

Classic Soba Noodles

If you want to be authentic, slurp noisily while eating these noodles. Look for any unfamiliar ingredients in Asian markets or well-stocked supermarkets. Wasabi is available prepared in a tube, or in powder form, which when mixed with water forms a paste. Mirin is a low-alcohol, slightly sweet rice wine.

8 oz. Japanese soba noodles
5 cups water
2 tsp. hon-dashi (fish-flavored soup
   base powder)
3 tbs. mirin or sake (rice wine)

wasabi (Japanese green horseradish)
   for garnish
minced green onion for garnish
grated fresh ginger for garnish

In a large pot of boiling water, cook soba noodles according to package directions until cooked through, but still slightly firm to the bite (*al dente*). Drain noodles and plunge into cold water to cool; set aside. In a medium saucepan, bring 5 cups water to a boil over high heat. Add hon-dashi and mirin and stir well.

To eat, place a portion of drained noodles on each serving plate. Place a small amount of wasabi, minced green onion and grated ginger on small condiment plates. Pour boiling hon-dashi mixture into warmed soup bowls. Let diners stir a small amount of each garnish into their portion of broth, pick up a strand or two of noodles with chopsticks, dip into broth and eat.

Cooking with Quinoa and Amaranth

About Quinoa and Amaranth

Quinoa and amaranth are small grains from South America. Both are highly nutritious, containing balanced protein, calcium and other minerals.

Quinoa

Quinoa (pronounced "KEEN-wah") was a staple food of the Incas for thousands of years. After their arrival, the Spaniards encouraged the cultivation of other grains with a higher yield, thus quinoa diminished in importance. Quinoa has recently experienced a resurgence in popularity, particularly for those on gluten-free diets.

Quinoa is not a "true" grain. Unlike true grains, quinoa has balanced amino acids and is considered to have a high protein content than any grain. While growing, individual grains of quinoa are covered with a natural, bitter-tasting coating, which protects it from insects and birds. Commercially available quinoa has usually been washed, but it is still a good idea to rinse the grains well before cooking.

Following are some popular forms of quinoa:

Whole-grain quinoa has a mild, delicate flavor and a slightly crunchy texture. The cooked grains are almost translucent. Cooked quinoa can substitute for rice in dishes and, like rice, it serves as a foil for strong flavors and seasonings.

Quinoa flour is made from ground quinoa grains. It lends a distinct flavor to baked goods and is made into pasta. In general, you can replace up to 25% of the wheat flour with quinoa flour in yeast breads.

Amaranth

The Aztecs believed amaranth to be as important as corn and beans for food. Vital to their culture, it provided energy for making superior warriors. With the death of Montezuma, Cortez commanded that the grain fields be burned. Amaranth was relegated to a minor status in the New World and never established a foothold in Europe. Rediscovered in the 1970s, amaranth is becoming more widely grown and available.

Amaranth is rich in protein, lysine, and calcium and other minerals. It has an aroma and flavor that reminds some people of celery.

Listed below are some popular forms of amaranth:

Whole-grain amaranth has a tendency to stick together, making it an ideal fat-free thickener for soups and sauces. Cooked amaranth quickly becomes quite firm upon cooling, but it can easily be reconstituted in the microwave.

Amaranth flour is made from ground amaranth seeds. In general, you can replace up to 25% of the wheat flour with amaranth flour in yeast breads.

Amaranth flakes make an interesting breakfast cereal and are perfect to use as a crunchy topping for a casserole.

Basic Cooked Quinoa

Toasting quinoa yields a richer flavor. If the recipe calls for toasted quinoa, place rinsed grains in a skillet over medium-high heat and stir until grains turn a darker shade of brown and smell toasted.

1 cup quinoa, rinsed   pinch salt
2 cups water or stock

Place quinoa in a sieve and rinse well under cold running water. Transfer to a medium saucepan with water and salt and bring to a boil over high heat. Cover pan, reduce heat to low and simmer for 10 to 15 minutes, until grains are translucent and the outer germ separates from grain. Drain any excess water and cool.

Basic Cooked Amaranth

Makes 2 cups

Amaranth cooks into a thick, creamy mixture, which is delicious in soups and stews. Cooked amaranth can be thinned to the desired consistency with water.

1 cup amaranth   pinch salt
3 cups cold water or stock

Place amaranth in a medium saucepan with water and salt and bring to a boil over high heat. Cover pan, reduce heat to low and simmer for 25 minutes, until grains are tender and liquid has been absorbed.

Quinoa Pecan Waffles

Cooked quinoa and chopped pecans add interesting flavor and texture to these crispy waffles.

¾ cup all-purpose flour
½ cup corn flour or rice flour
2 tsp. baking soda
1 tsp. baking powder
½ tsp. salt
3 large eggs, separated

3 tbs. vegetable oil
1 tbs. honey
2 cups buttermilk
1 cup *Basic Cooked Quinoa*, page 132
⅓ cup chopped pecans

Heat waffle iron. In a large bowl, combine flours, soda, baking powder and salt and stir well. In a small bowl, whisk egg yolks until lemon-colored and stir in oil, honey and buttermilk. Pour egg mixture into flour mixture and stir just to combine. Stir in quinoa and pecans. In another bowl, beat egg whites until stiff peaks form and fold into batter. Spray waffle grids with nonstick cooking spray. Bake waffles according to manufacturer's instructions for your waffle iron.

Amaranth-Applesauce Muffins

Applesauce adds flavor and gives these easy-to-put-together muffins a tender, moist texture.

¼ cup butter, softened
½ cup brown sugar, packed
1 large egg
1 cup applesauce
1 cup all-purpose flour
1 cup amaranth flour

2 tsp. baking powder
½ tsp. salt
1½ tsp. cinnamon
¼ tsp. nutmeg
¼ tsp. ground cloves
½ cup raisins

Heat oven to 400°. Butter a 12-cup muffin tin and set aside. With a mixer, beat butter and sugar until light and fluffy. Add egg and beat well. Stir in applesauce. In another bowl, sift together flours, baking powder, salt, 1 tsp. of the cinnamon, nutmeg and cloves. Add flour mixture to applesauce mixture and stir just to moisten dry ingredients. Fold in raisins, taking care not to overmix batter. Spoon batter into muffin cups and sprinkle tops of muffins with remaining ½ tsp. cinnamon. Bake for 18 to 20 minutes, until a toothpick inserted into the center of a muffin comes out clean.

Quinoa, Carrot and Tahini Dip

Scoop up this full-flavored dip with pita chips or pieces of carrot, turnip, jicama or celery. The dip keeps well in the refrigerator for a few days.

1¼ cups water
½ cup quinoa, rinsed
2 carrots, peeled and coarsely grated
4 cloves roasted garlic
¼ cup tahini or Asian sesame paste
¼ cup lemon juice
½ tsp. ground cumin

2-3 drops Tabasco Sauce, optional
¼ tsp. salt
freshly ground pepper to taste
1-2 tbs. water, if needed
paprika for garnish
chopped fresh cilantro or parsley for
  garnish

In a medium saucepan, bring water to a boil. In a dry skillet, toast quinoa over medium heat for 3 to 4 minutes, until lightly browned. Transfer quinoa with carrots to pan with boiling water. Cover pan, reduce heat to low and simmer for 18 minutes, until quinoa is soft and liquid has been absorbed. Remove from heat and let stand covered for a few minutes. Transfer mixture to a food processor workbowl and process until smooth. Add garlic, tahini, lemon juice, cumin, Tabasco, salt and pepper and pulse several times to blend well. Adjust seasonings and transfer to a serving bowl. Chill mixture until about 30 minutes before serving. Thin with 1 to 2 tbs. water, if needed, to reach dipping consistency. Garnish with paprika and cilantro.

Creamy Corn and Quinoa Soup

Make this soup the day before you serve it and present it as a first course for a summer dinner party. For a different accent, garnish it with fresh cilantro and thin lime slices, or dollops of fresh tomato and avocado salsa. Amaranth or millet can be substituted for the quinoa.

1 tbs. vegetable oil
1 cup diced onion
1 large jalapeño chile, stemmed, seeded and minced
kernels from 4 large ears fresh sweet corn, or
    2 pkg. (10 oz. each) frozen corn
3 cups water
3 cups *Basic Chicken Stock*, page 8, or canned chicken broth
½ cup quinoa, rinsed
salt and freshly ground pepper to taste
2 tbs. fresh lime juice
1 tbs. butter
sweet basil leaves cut into ribbons for garnish

In a stockpot, heat oil over medium heat. Add onion and jalapeño and sauté for 3 to 4 minutes. Reserve ½ cup corn kernels for garnish. Add remaining corn to skillet and cook for 2 to 3 minutes. Add water and bring to a boil over high heat. Cover pot, reduce heat to low and simmer for 20 minutes, until vegetables are tender. Remove pot from heat and cool for a few minutes.

Process vegetables with a food processor and strain through a coarse sieve. Return smooth vegetable mixture to stockpot, add chicken stock and bring to a boil over high heat. Stir in quinoa, salt and pepper. Reduce heat to low and simmer for 20 minutes, until quinoa is translucent. Add lime juice and adjust seasonings.

In a small saucepan, heat butter over medium-low heat and sauté reserved ½ cup corn kernels for 3 to 4 minutes, until tender. Ladle soup into warm bowls and garnish each serving with a spoonful of sautéed corn and a few ribbons of basil. Serve immediately.

Leek, Potato and Amaranth Soup

*It takes less than an hour to make this soup. It is delicious on its own, or it can be used as a base for **Clam Chowder** or **Vichyssoise**, page 139. Use the thin slicing blade on the food processor to slice the potatoes.*

3 tbs. butter
3 large leeks, white part only, well washed and coarsely chopped (about 4 cups)
2 medium stalks celery, thinly sliced
½ cup amaranth
2-3 cups sliced peeled potatoes (about 2 large, or 1½ lb.)
4 cups *Basic Chicken Stock*, page 8, or canned chicken broth
3 cups water
salt and finely ground white pepper to taste
chopped fresh parsley or chives for garnish

In a large heavy stockpot, melt butter over medium heat. Add leeks and celery and sauté for 5 to 6 minutes, until softened. Stir in amaranth. Add sliced potatoes, chicken stock and water and bring to a boil over high heat. Cover pot, reduce heat to low and simmer for about 40 minutes. Cool soup for a few minutes. With a food processor or blender, carefully puree hot soup in batches and return to pot. Season with salt and pepper, heat through and garnish with chopped parsley.

138   Cooking with Quinoa and Amaranth

Vichyssoise

Serve this as a first course for a summer evening dinner.

4 cups *Leek, Potato and Amaranth Soup*, page 139, cooled
½ cup heavy cream
chopped fresh chives for garnish

To cold soup, add cream and stir well. Chill for several hours in the refrigerator. Serve very cold garnished with chopped chives.

Clam Chowder

Strain clam juice through a coffee filter or paper towel to catch any sand.

4 cups hot *Leek, Potato and Amaranth Soup*, page 138
2 cans (6½ oz. each) chopped clams with juice
¼ tsp. Tabasco Sauce
chopped fresh parsley for garnish

To hot soup, add clams, clam juice and Tabasco; stir well and heat through. Serve garnished with parsley.

Green Chile-Amaranth Soup

In this creamy, mildly spicy soup, amaranth provides richness without adding fat. Serve the soup as a first course for a special dinner party. If making it ahead of time and reheating, thin it to the desired consistency with stock or water.

1 tbs. butter
6 green onions, white part only, thinly
   sliced
1 can (4 oz.) whole roasted green
   chiles, drained
½ cup amaranth
salt to taste

¼ tsp. white pepper
3 cups *Basic Chicken Stock*, page 8,
   or canned chicken broth
2 tbs. dry sherry
cilantro leaves or diced roasted red bell
   pepper for garnish

In a large saucepan, melt butter over medium heat and sauté onions for 3 to 4 minutes, until softened. Remove stems and seeds from chiles, chop coarsely and add to saucepan with amaranth; stir briefly. Add salt, pepper and stock and bring to a boil over high heat. Reduce heat to low and simmer uncovered for 40 minutes. Remove from heat and cool for a few minutes. With a blender or food processor, carefully puree hot soup in batches and return to pan. Stir in sherry, adjust seasonings and heat soup through. Serve hot garnished with cilantro or red pepper.

Quinoa Salad with Roasted Corn, Mango and Black Beans

This colorful salad boasts a lively curry and lime vinaigrette. Serve it as an accompaniment to grilled meats or as part of a salad buffet. Substitute couscous or kasha for the quinoa, if you like.

kernels from 3 ears fresh sweet corn
  (about 2 cups)
5 tbs. vegetable oil
salt and freshly ground pepper to taste
½ cup finely chopped red onion
1 jalapeño chile, stemmed, seeded
  and minced

1 tsp. Madras curry powder
1½ cups *Basic Cooked Quinoa*,
  page 132
1 can (15 oz.) black beans, rinsed and
  drained
1 ripe mango, peeled and diced
1 lime

Heat oven to 425°. Line a rimmed baking sheet with foil. Toss corn with 2 tbs. of the oil, salt and pepper and spread in a single layer on baking sheet. Bake for 15 to 18 minutes, stirring once or twice, until corn is lightly browned; cool slightly. In a small skillet, heat remaining 3 tbs. vegetable oil over low heat. Add onion and jalapeño and sauté for 4 to 5 minutes, until onion is soft and translucent. Stir in curry powder and cook for 1 minute. In a bowl, combine roasted corn, onion mixture, quinoa, beans and mango. Squeeze lime juice over salad and season with salt and pepper.

Eggplant and Squash Gratin

Garden vegetables are baked with a garlic, herb, cheese and amaranth topping. Serve this dish as an accompaniment to grilled meats or as part of a salad and vegetable buffet. You can make this dish ahead of time and reheat it just before serving.

⅓ cup plus 2 tbs. full-flavored olive oil
1 large onion, thinly sliced
1 large red bell pepper, peeled and thinly sliced
salt and freshly ground pepper to taste
4 Asian eggplants (about 1 lb.), trimmed and cut into ¼-inch slices
2 medium zucchini, trimmed and cut into ¼-inch slices
2 yellow crookneck squash, trimmed and cut into ¼-inch slices
3 cloves garlic, finely chopped
1 tbs. fresh thyme leaves
12 leaves fresh sweet basil, cut into ribbons
1 cup crumbled feta cheese
1 cup lightly crushed amaranth flakes

In a medium skillet, heat 2 tbs. olive oil over medium heat. Add onion slices and sauté for about 5 minutes, until soft and translucent. Add red pepper and continue to cook for 3 to 5 minutes, until soft. Season with salt and pepper.

Heat oven to 375°. Lightly oil a shallow ovenproof baking dish. Spoon about ⅔ of the onion-pepper mixture into dish. Starting with eggplant, arrange 1 row of slices around the edge of baking dish, standing them up against edge of pan. In the same manner, arrange a a row of zucchini slices followed by yellow squash slices, alternating colors. Continue with a row of eggplant slices and finish with squash slices. Spoon remaining ⅓ of the onion-pepper mixture over the top.

In a medium bowl, whisk garlic and herbs with ⅓ cup olive oil. Stir in feta cheese and amaranth flakes and season with salt and pepper. Pour feta mixture evenly over vegetables. Cover pan with foil and bake for 40 minutes. Remove foil and continue to bake for 20 minutes, until vegetables are very soft and topping is nicely browned. Serve warm or at room temperature.

Manicotti

Preformed manicotti shells are stuffed with a savory ricotta and quinoa filling and covered with a rich tomato sauce. Bake it in individual gratin dishes or 1 large baking pan. Accompany the manicotti with a crisp green salad, garlic bread and your choice of red or white wine.

2 tbs. olive oil
1 large onion, finely chopped
2 cloves garlic, minced
2 cans (14 oz. each) ready-cut tomatoes
1 tsp. dried oregano
1/4 cup chopped fresh basil
pinch red pepper flakes
salt and freshly ground pepper to taste
1 pkg. (8 oz.) preformed manicotti shells
1 1/4 cups ricotta cheese
2 cups *Basic Cooked Quinoa* or *Basic Cooked Amaranth*, page 132
1 1/4 cups grated fontina or Swiss cheese
3 tbs. slivered sun-dried tomatoes
1/2 cup freshly grated Parmesan cheese
1/4 cup chopped fresh parsley
salt and freshly ground pepper to taste

In a medium skillet, heat olive oil over medium heat and sauté onion for 5 to 7 minutes, until soft. Add garlic and sauté for 1 minute. Transfer ½ of the onion mixture to a plate and set aside.

Place tomatoes in a food processor workbowl or blender container and pulse several times, until coarsely chopped. To skillet, add tomatoes, oregano, basil, pepper flakes, salt and pepper. Simmer mixture uncovered for 15 to 20 minutes, until slightly thickened.

Bring a large pot of water to a rolling boil and cook manicotti shells according to package directions, about 8 minutes. Drain manicotti shells and rinse under warm water; blot dry on paper towels. In a bowl, combine reserved onion mixture, ricotta, quinoa, fontina, sun-dried tomatoes, ¼ cup of the Parmesan cheese, parsley, salt and pepper; mix well.

Heat oven to 375°. Pour a thin layer of tomato sauce in a large baking dish. With a teaspoon, fill manicotti shells with ricotta filling and arrange in baking dish. Top filled shells with remaining tomato sauce and sprinkle with remaining ¼ cup Parmesan cheese. Cover pan and bake for about 20 minutes, until hot and bubbling. Serve on warm plates.

Quinoa Pasta with Vegetables

Deep yellow quinoa pasta spirals are paired with a creamy mushroom sauce that can be made in the time it takes to bring the pasta water to a boil.

1 tbs. salt
12 oz. quinoa pasta spirals
2 tbs. full-flavored olive oil
1/2 cup chopped red or yellow onion
3/4 lb. cremini (brown) mushrooms, trimmed and thinly sliced
1/2 tsp. red pepper flakes

leaves from 2 sprigs fresh thyme, or 1/2 tsp. dried
1/3 cup slivered sun-dried tomatoes
1/4 cup heavy cream
salt and freshly ground pepper to taste
1/4 cup chopped fresh parsley
grated Parmesan cheese

Bring a large pot of water to a boil and add salt and pasta. Cook for about 8 minutes, until cooked through, but still slightly firm to the bite (*al dente*). While pasta is cooking, heat oil in a large skillet over medium heat. Add onions and sauté for 3 to 4 minutes, until softened. Add mushrooms and pepper flakes and cook for 2 to 3 minutes, until mushroom liquid is released. Add thyme, tomatoes, cream, salt and pepper. Bring mixture to a boil and cook for 1 minute. Drain pasta, add to skillet with sauce and toss to coat. Thin sauce with 1 to 2 tbs. pasta cooking water, if necessary. Sprinkle with parsley and serve immediately. Pass Parmesan.

Gingerbread

This spicy cake travels well and makes great lunchbox or picnic fare.

⅓ cup butter, softened, or vegetable shortening
½ cup brown sugar, packed
1 large egg
⅔ cup molasses
1 cup amaranth flour
1 cup all-purpose flour
1 tsp. baking soda

1 tsp. baking powder
½ tsp. salt
2 tsp. ground ginger
1 tsp. cinnamon
¼ tsp. ground cloves
¾ cup buttermilk
confectioners' sugar

Heat oven to 350°. Butter a 9-x-9-inch baking pan. With a mixer, beat butter and sugar until light and fluffy. Add egg and mix well. Stir in molasses. In another bowl, sift together flours, baking soda, baking powder, salt, ginger, cinnamon and cloves. Gradually add flour mixture to butter mixture alternately with buttermilk, stirring between additions. Pour batter into prepared pan and bake for 40 to 45 minutes, until gingerbread pulls away from the sides of pan and a toothpick inserted into the center comes out clean. Cool on a rack. Sift a small amount of confectioners' sugar over gingerbread before serving.

Cooking with Other Grains:
Kamut, Rye, Triticale and Flax

About Kamut, Rye, Triticale and Flax

Many unusual grains are available in specialty markets and health food stores, and provide interesting and healthful additions to our daily diet.

Kamut

Kamut (pronounced "kah-MOOT") is an ancient Egyptian form of wheat with kernels 2 to 3 times larger than regular wheat. Although kamut does contain gluten, some people who are sensitive to wheat can eat it.

Whole-grain kamut can be substituted for wheat berries in most recipes.

Kamut flakes, a cereal form of kamut, can be used in baking or for a crispy topping for a gratin or casserole.

Rye

Rye can be grown in cold, damp climates where wheat does not grow well, such as Russia, Scandinavia and Eastern Europe. Rye has a slight gray hue and tangy taste.

Rye berries can be substituted for wheat, spelt or triticale berries in recipes.

Rye flour, commonly used in pumpernickel and rye breads, contains little gluten. In general, you can replace up to 50% of the wheat flour with rye flour in yeast breads to make nice, light breads with good rye flavor.

Triticale

Triticale (pronounced "tri-ti-CAY-lee") is a cross between wheat and rye that thrives in cold, damp climates where wheat doesn't grow well.

Triticale berries are similar to wheat berries, only smaller. You can substitute triticale berries for wheat berries, rye berries, brown rice or pearl barley in recipes.

Triticale flour has a small amount of gluten which, if using exclusively in bread recipes, requires more gentle kneading and only one rising period.

Flax

Flax has been cultivated to make linen fiber since the time of the Egyptian mummies. Today, a second strain of flax is produced for oil and food. Research suggests that flax may provide beneficial nutrients. Flax provides soluble fiber, Omega-3 fatty acids and high-quality protein. Use caution when using flax in cooking as, like wheat and other grains, some people are allergic to it. Flax is used for baked goods and crackers or it can be added to cooked vegetable dishes or grain salads.

Whole flaxseed can be ground in a coffee or spice mill as you need it.

Milled flaxseed is available, but doesn't keep as long as whole flaxseed. Store milled flaxseed in the refrigerator and use within a few weeks.

Basic Cooked Kamut

Do not add salt to kamut while cooking; doing so could increase the cooking time and/or toughen the grains.

1 cup kamut
3 cups cold water, plus water to cover

Place kamut in a medium saucepan and cover with water; cover pan and let stand for 6 to 8 hours, or overnight. *Quick soak method*: Place kamut in a medium saucepan, cover with water and bring to a boil. Cover pan, remove from heat and let stand for 1 hour; drain.

In a saucepan, bring 3 cups cold water to a boil over high heat. Add soaked kamut. Cover pan, reduce heat to low and simmer for 45 to 50 minutes, until kamut is tender.

Basic Cooked Rye or Triticale Berries

Rye berries and triticale berries are very sturdy and require lengthy cooking times. If buying berries in bulk, carefully sort through them to remove any small stones or debris. Rinse rye or triticale berries well in cold water before using. Do not salt the berries until after they are cooked, as salt slows down the absorption of liquid into the grain.

1 cup rye or triticale berries
3 cups cold water, plus water to cover

Place rye or triticale berries in a large bowl and cover with cold water. Let stand covered overnight; drain. *Quick Soak Method*: Place berries in a medium saucepan, cover with water and bring to a boil. Remove from heat and let stand for 1 hour; drain.

In a medium saucepan, bring 3 cups water to a boil over high heat. Add soaked rye or triticale berries. Reduce heat to low, cover pan and simmer for about 30 to 45 minutes, until tender.

Flax-Multigrain Crackers

Flavorful and crunchy, these crackers are easy to mix and bake. Serve them with soup or as a snack with cheddar cheese.

1¼ cups bread flour
¾ cup kamut or corn flour
¼ cup milled flaxseed, plus extra for topping
1 tsp. baking powder
¾ tsp. salt

½ tsp. chili powder, optional
1 tbs. sugar
¼ cup vegetable shortening, divided into 3-4 pieces
½ cup milk
kosher salt for topping, optional

Heat oven to 325°. Lightly oil baking sheets or line with parchment paper. In a food processor workbowl, combine flours, flaxseed, baking powder, salt, chili powder, if using, and sugar. Pulse 2 to 3 times to mix ingredients. Add shortening and pulse several times, until mixture resembles coarse meal. With the motor running, add milk and process until dough forms a ball and cleans the sides of bowl. Divide dough into 2 equal pieces. On a floured surface, roll each piece into a ⅛-inch-thick rectangle. Lightly sprinkle dough with flaxseed and kosher salt, if desired. With rolling pin, press toppings into dough. With a pizza cutter or knife, cut dough into 1½-inch squares. Place squares on baking sheets and bake for 20 to 25 minutes, turning over halfway through baking time, until crisp and lightly browned. Cool and store in anairtight container.

Cranberry Batter Bread

This slightly sweet bread features dried cranberries and nuts. Serve it warm, at room temperature or cut into slices and toasted. This bread freezes well.

⅓ cup organic triticale, wheat or amaranth flakes
1 cup kamut flour
2¼ cups all-purpose flour
½ tsp. cinnamon
½ tsp. mace
1 tsp. salt
½ cup sugar

1½ tsp. baking powder
¼ cup butter, cut into 4 pieces
1¾ cups milk
2 large eggs, lightly beaten
1 tsp. vanilla extract
1 cup dried cranberries
1 cup chopped toasted walnuts

Heat oven to 350°. Butter an 8-x-8-x-2½-inch pan and set aside. In a large bowl, combine triticale flakes, flours, cinnamon, mace, salt, sugar and baking powder and stir until mixed. In a small saucepan, heat butter and milk over medium heat until butter melts. Pour hot milk mixture into flour mixture and stir until mixed. Add eggs and vanilla and mix well. Stir in cranberries and walnuts, taking care not to overmix batter. Spoon batter into prepared baking pan. Bake for 55 to 60 minutes, until top is lightly browned and a toothpick inserted into the center comes out clean. Cool on a rack.

Whole Wheat Flax Bread

Flaxseed adds a wonderful nutty taste to this whole wheat bread, which is delicious toasted or used for sandwiches.

1⅔ cups milk
2 tbs. butter
3 tbs. honey or brown sugar
1½ tsp. salt
1 pkg. active dry yeast

1 cup whole wheat flour
2 cups bread flour
¾ cup milled flaxseed
melted butter for brushing

Generously butter a 9-x-5-inch loaf pan. In a small saucepan over medium heat, heat milk, butter, honey and salt until butter melts. Remove from heat and cool to 105° to 110°. Add yeast and stir to dissolve. In a mixer bowl fitted with the paddle attachment, combine flours and flaxseed. With the motor running on medium speed, gradually add warm milk mixture to flour mixture and mix for about 2 minutes; dough will be sticky. Spoon dough into prepared pan, cover with plastic wrap and let rise in a warm place until doubled in size, about 1½ hours.

Heat oven to 350°. Brush top of bread with a small amount of melted butter. Bake bread for about 70 minutes, until the internal temperature reads 206° to 210° on an instant-read thermometer. Cool on a rack.

Scandinavian Orange Rye Bread

Rye and kamut flours lend their wholesome flavors to this orange- and anise-scented bread. Bake it in rounds or in 9-x-5-inch loaf pans. When baking bread, you may not need to use all of the flour called for in the recipe, depending on the ingredients used and the climate in which you are baking. Practice making bread and you will learn how bread dough should feel when it is ready.

1 tsp. anise seeds
1 tsp. cumin seeds
1 tsp. fennel seeds
grated peel (zest) and juice of 1 orange
water
2 pkg. active dry yeast
1½ cups rye flour
1½ cups kamut flour
⅓ cup dark corn syrup
2 tsp. sugar
2 tsp. salt
3 tbs. butter, softened
3-4 cups bread flour

With a spice grinder or mortar and pestle, grind anise, cumin and fennel seeds to a fine powder; set aside. Place orange juice in a liquid measuring cup and add enough water to equal 2 cups. Heat liquid to about 105°. Pour warm liquid into a mixer bowl, sprinkle yeast over liquid and stir in 1 cup of the rye flour. Let stand for about 10 minutes, until bubbly. With mixer's paddle attachment, beat in remaining ½ cup rye flour, kamut flour, corn syrup, sugar, ground seeds, orange zest and salt until smooth, about 2 minutes. Add softened butter and mix well. Replace paddle attachment with mixer's dough hook and gradually knead in about 3 cups of the bread flour, ½ cup at a time. Mix on medium speed until dough comes together and cleans the side of bowl. Transfer dough to a floured work surface and finish kneading by hand, using some of the remaining flour, until dough is smooth and elastic. Form dough into a ball and place in a large oiled bowl. Turn dough to coat all sides lightly with oil. Cover bowl with plastic wrap and let dough rise in a warm place until doubled in size, about 1¼ hours. Punch down dough and divide in half. Oil a baking sheet or 2 bread pans. Shape dough into round balls if baking on a sheet, or form into loaves and place in bread pans. Cover dough lightly with plastic wrap and let rise until doubled in size, about 1 hour.

Heat oven to 375°. Slash top of loaves with a sharp knife or razor blade. Bake for about 45 minutes, until the internal temperature reads 206° to 210° on an instant-read thermometer. Cool on a rack.

Walnut, Roasted Garlic and Triticale Bread

Makes 1 loaf

The walnut and roasted garlic flavors make this bread perfect to serve for a cheese course. Or, slice it thinly and make it into a sandwich filled with grilled eggplant and red peppers.

¾ cup buttermilk, warmed to 105°
1 pkg. active-dry yeast
1 cup walnuts, toasted
2½ cups bread flour
½ cup soaked triticale berries (see page 152),
    drained and patted dry
1½ tsp. salt
1 tsp. brown sugar
3 tbs. walnut or olive oil, plus 1 tsp. for brushing
Roasted Garlic, follows

Place warmed buttermilk in a bowl and sprinkle with yeast; let stand for 10 minutes. With a food processor, process walnuts until finely ground; set aside. Add ½ cup of the bread flour and soaked triticale berries and process until berries are finely ground. Add remaining 2 cups flour, salt, brown sugar, 3 tbs. walnut oil, *Roasted Garlic* and walnuts and pulse 2 to 3 times to mix. With motor running, slowly add buttermilk mixture and process for 30 to 45 seconds, until dough forms sticky ball.

Transfer dough to a lightly floured work surface and knead in a little flour. Form dough into a ball and place in a large oiled bowl. Turn dough to coat all sides lightly with oil. Cover bowl with plastic wrap and let dough rise in a warm place until doubled in size, about 1¼ hours.

Punch down dough and transfer to a floured work surface. Shape dough into a loaf about 12 inches long and place on an oiled or parchment-lined baking sheet. Cover dough lightly with plastic wrap and let rise until doubled, about 1 hour.

Heat oven to 400°. Place bread in oven and immediately reduce oven temperature to 350°. Bake bread for about 1 hour, until the internal temperature reads 206° to 210° on an instant-read thermometer. Cool on a rack.

Roasted Garlic
Makes about 3-4 tablespoons

1 bulb garlic
1 tsp. olive oil

Heat oven to 350°. Cut off about ½ inch from the top of garlic bulb, slicing off a little of the individual cloves. Place on a small sheet of aluminum foil and drizzle with olive oil. Wrap garlic tightly in foil and bake for 35 to 40 minutes, or until garlic is soft. Remove foil and cool. Squeeze garlic pulp from garlic cloves and mash with a fork.

Kamut and Bean Soup

Traditional flavors of Mexico complement this hearty soup. If you like, add some diced cooked chicken at the very end and cook the soup for another 5 minutes. You can substitute cooked wheat berries or rye berries for kamut, if desired.

2 tbs. vegetable oil
1 large onion, finely chopped
2 carrots, peeled and finely diced
2 cloves garlic, finely chopped
1 canned chipotle chile, stemmed,
   seeded and finely chopped
½ tsp. dried oregano
1 tsp. ground cumin
2 cups *Basic Cooked Kamut*, page 151
1 can (14 oz.) ready-cut tomatoes

2½ cups *Basic Chicken Stock*, page 8,
   or canned chicken broth
salt and freshly ground pepper to taste
1 can (15 oz.) pinto beans, rinsed and
   drained
1 tbs. lime juice
fresh cilantro leaves for garnish
1 cup shredded Monterey Jack cheese
   for garnish
lime wedges

In a heavy 3-quart saucepan, heat oil over medium-low heat and sauté onion and carrots for 8 to 10 minutes, until soft. Add garlic, chipotle, oregano and cumin and cook for 2 to 3 minutes. Add kamut and toss to coat well. Add tomatoes, stock, salt and pepper and bring to a boil over high heat. Reduce heat to low and simmer uncovered for 15 minutes. Add beans and heat through. Stir in lime juice. Serve in warm soup bowls garnished with cilantro. Pass cheese and limes.

Caramelized Onion and Potato Gratin

The potatoes can be boiled or baked for this gratin, which can be assembled ahead of time and baked just before serving. Kamut flakes provide a wonderful crunch to the crispy topping.

2 lb. Yukon gold or russet potatoes,
   cooked and peeled
1 cup buttermilk
salt and freshly ground pepper to taste

2 tbs. full-flavored olive oil
1 large onion, coarsely chopped
¾ cup kamut flakes
2 tbs. freshly grated Parmesan cheese

Mash cooked potatoes or run through a ricer. Place mashed potatoes in a bowl and gradually add buttermilk, beating until smooth. Season with salt and pepper. In a medium skillet, heat olive oil over medium-low heat and sauté onion for 10 to 15 minutes, until lightly browned and soft. Add kamut flakes and Parmesan cheese and toss to thoroughly mix with onion and olive oil.

Heat oven to 375°. Oil a 8-x-8-inch baking pan. Spread potato mixture evenly in pan and top with kamut-onion mixture. Bake for 25 to 30 minutes, until potatoes are heated through and topping is lightly browned. Serve hot.

Kamut and Red Lentils

Serve this colorful melange as a side dish with roasted chicken or grilled fish. Wheat or rye berries can be substituted for kamut. Red lentils cook very quickly and add a bright color to the dish. Ghee is another word for clarified butter. Look for it in jars in Indian or Middle Eastern markets.

½ cup red lentils, rinsed
1½ cups water
2 tbs. butter or ghee
1 medium onion, finely chopped
1 clove garlic, finely chopped
1 tsp. curry powder

1½ cups *Basic Cooked Kamut*,
   page 151
1 cup fresh or thawed frozen peas
salt and freshly ground pepper to taste
1 tbs. lemon juice
2 tbs. chopped fresh parsley

In a medium saucepan, combine lentils and water and bring to a boil over high heat. Cover pan, reduce heat to low and simmer for 5 to 7 minutes, until lentils are tender. Drain any remaining liquid.

In a medium skillet, melt butter over low heat and sauté onion for 8 to 10 minutes, until very soft. Add garlic and curry powder and cook for 1 minute. Stir in kamut and cooked lentils. Add peas, salt and pepper and sauté for 5 minutes, until peas are cooked and mixture is hot. Stir in lemon juice, sprinkle with parsley and serve.

Rye Berries with Mushrooms and Snow Peas

Serve this as a flavorful side dish with duck or chicken. Substitute wheat berries or brown rice for rye berries, if desired.

2 tbs. butter
8-10 cremini (brown) mushrooms,
    trimmed and thinly sliced
1 bunch green onions, white part only, thinly sliced
1 tsp. dried tarragon
1 tbs. soy sauce
1 tbs. dry sherry or lemon juice
2 cups *Basic Cooked Rye Berries*, page 152
12-15 snow peas, strings removed and cut on the diagonal into ½-inch pieces
salt and freshly ground pepper to taste

In a medium skillet, melt butter over medium-high heat and sauté mushrooms for 3 to 4 minutes. Add onions and sauté for 2 to 3 minutes. Add tarragon, soy sauce, sherry and rye berries and mix well. Stir in snow peas, salt and pepper. Cover pan, reduce heat to medium-low and simmer for 2 to 3 minutes, until snow peas are crisp-tender. Serve immediately.

Onion Tart with Rye Crust

Sweet "melted" onions and tangy cheese fill a savory rye crust. Serve wedges of this tart with lightly dressed salad greens on the side. Make the pastry first and cook the onions while the pastry is chilling.

¾ cup all-purpose flour
½ cup rye flour
½ tsp. salt
6 tbs. chilled butter, cut into 6 pieces

2 tbs. plain yogurt or sour cream
1-2 tbs. ice water
Onion Filling, follows

In a food processor workbowl, combine flours and salt. Add butter and pulse 6 or 7 times, until butter is size of small peas. Add yogurt and 1 tbs. ice water. Process until mixture starts to form a ball, adding additional water if dough is too dry to hold together. Form dough into a flat round, wrap in plastic wrap and refrigerate for 1 hour.

Heat oven to 400°. Place dough between 2 sheets of waxed paper and roll out to a 12-inch circle. Place in a 9-x-2½-inch tart pan with a removable bottom, allowing dough to come up the sides. Cover dough with aluminum foil and fill with pie weights or dried beans. Bake for 15 minutes. Remove foil and weights and continue to bake for 2 to 3 minutes, until crust feels dry to the touch. Cool on a rack.

Pour *Onion Filling* into cooled crust. Reduce oven temperature to 375° and bake tart for about 1 hour, until filling is puffed and lightly browned. Serve warm or at room temperature.

Onion Filling
3 large onions, about 1½ lb.
2 tbs. butter
½ tsp. dried thyme
¼ cup dry vermouth
1 tbs. balsamic vinegar
4 large eggs
⅔ cup shredded Gruyère cheese
salt and freshly ground pepper to taste

Peel onions, cut into quarters and thinly slice crosswise. In a large skillet over medium heat, melt butter. Add sliced onions and sauté for 5 to 6 minutes, taking care not to let onions brown. Add thyme and vermouth. Cover pan and cook over very low heat for 25 to 30 minutes, stirring once or twice, until onions are very soft. If onions start to stick to pan, add a little water. Remove lid, increase heat to medium and cook until any liquid in pan has evaporated. Stir in balsamic vinegar and remove from heat. Cool for at least 5 minutes. In a large bowl, whisk eggs. Stir in grated cheese and onions. Season mixture with salt and pepper.

Walnut Flax Drop Cookies

Makes about 6 dozen

Pack these sweet, crisp cookies as a lunchbox treat or serve them as an accompaniment to coffee or tea. Store extras in an airtight container.

1⅓ cups all-purpose flour
1 tsp. baking powder
½ tsp. baking soda
¼ tsp. freshly grated nutmeg
⅛ tsp. salt
⅓ cup milled flaxseed

⅓ cup shortening
⅓ cup butter, softened
1½ cups brown sugar, packed
1 large egg
½ tsp. vanilla extract
⅔ cup chopped toasted walnuts

Heat oven to 350°. Lightly oil baking sheets or line with parchment paper. In a medium bowl, combine flour, baking powder, baking soda, nutmeg, salt and flaxseed and stir until mixed. With a mixer, beat shortening, butter and sugar until light and fluffy. Add egg and vanilla and beat well. Gradually add flour mixture to butter mixture, mixing just until combined. Stir in walnuts. Drop cookie dough by heaping teaspoonfuls onto baking sheets about 2 inches apart. Bake for 12 to 15 minutes, until lightly browned and firm to the touch. Cool on a rack.

INDEX

Serve creative, easy, nutritious meals with nitty gritty® cookbooks

Wraps and Roll-Ups
Easy Vegetarian Cooking
Party Fare: Irresistible Nibbles
   for Every Occasion
Cappuccino/Espresso: The Book of
   Beverages
Fresh Vegetables
Cooking with Fresh Herbs
Cooking with Chile Peppers
The Dehydrator Cookbook
Recipes for the Pressure Cooker
Beer and Good Food
Unbeatable Chicken Recipes
Gourmet Gifts
From Freezer, 'Fridge and Pantry
Edible Pockets for Every Meal
Oven and Rotisserie Roasting
Risottos, Paellas and Other Rice
   Specialties
Muffins, Nut Breads and More
Healthy Snacks for Kids
100 Dynamite Desserts
Recipes for Yogurt Cheese
Sautés
Cooking in Porcelain

Casseroles
The Toaster Oven Cookbook
Skewer Cooking on the Grill
Creative Mexican Cooking
Marinades
No Salt, No Sugar, No Fat Cookbook
Quick and Easy Pasta Recipes
Cooking in Clay
Deep Fried Indulgences
The Garlic Cookbook
From Your Ice Cream Maker
The Best Pizza is Made at Home
The Best Bagels are Made at Home
Convection Oven Cookery
The Steamer Cookbook
The Pasta Machine Cookbook
The Versatile Rice Cooker
The Bread Machine Cookbook
The Bread Machine Cookbook II
The Bread Machine Cookbook III
The Bread Machine Cookbook IV:
   Whole Grains & Natural Sugars
The Bread Machine Cookbook V:
   *Favorite Recipes from 100
   Kitchens*

The Bread Machine Cookbook VI:
   *Hand-Shaped Breads from the
   Dough Cycle*
Worldwide Sourdoughs from Your
   Bread Machine
Entrées from Your Bread Machine
The New Blender Book
The Sandwich Maker Cookbook
Waffles
The Coffee Book
The Juicer Book I and II
Bread Baking
The 9 x 13 Pan Cookbook
Recipes for the Loaf Pan
Low Fat American Favorites
Healthy Cooking on the Run
Favorite Seafood Recipes
New International Fondue Cookbook
Favorite Cookie Recipes
Cooking for 1 or 2
The Well Dressed Potato
Extra-Special Crockery Pot Recipes
Slow Cooking
The Wok

For a free catalog, write or call: Bristol Publishing Enterprises, Inc.
P.O. Box 1737, San Leandro, CA 94577 (800) 346-4889